A

HISTORY OF FOX-HUNTING

IN THE WYNNSTAY COUNTRY AND
PART OF SHROPSHIRE,

*From the Beginning of this Century to the End of the
Season of 1884-85.*

BY

T H G Puleston

1893.

LADY WILLIAMS WYNN.

To LOUISE ALEXANDRA

LADY WILLIAMS WYNN.

THIS VOLUME IS DEDICATED OUT OF REGARD

FOR HERSELF AND IN MEMORY OF A

LIFE-LONG FRIENDSHIP WITH

HER FATHER, BY

—THE AUTHOR.

SIR WATKIN W. WYNN.

PREFACE.

HAVING written the following pages only at the request of a friend, I ask for an indulgent judgment of my work, from those neighbours who have generously taken on trust, my powers of dealing efficiently with my subject.

I have endeavoured to establish the accuracy of all the facts and dates which I have given, but have not attempted to fix the time when the several members of the hunt whom I have named began or finished their hunting career. I shall feel myself amply recompensed for my trouble if these pages keep green, even for a time, the memory of our late M.F.H., Sir W. W. Wynn, to whose generosity the country is indebted for the sport of fox hunting for more than forty years, and whose hospitality was shared by every resident in the country.

July 4th, 1893.

THE
WYNNSTAY COUNTRY.

———— :o: ————

CHAPTER I.

" When time, which steals our hours away,
Shall steal our pleasures too,
The memory of the past shall stay
And half our joys renew."

—MOORE.

Probably some who take an interest in fox hunting may be surprised to hear how modern, com-
paratively speaking. the sport is, and under what
different conditions it was formerly pursued.

As far as we can learn, there is no record of any
pack of hounds being used exclusively for hunting
the fox in this part of England or Wales before the
year 1772. Hounds were kept in many parts of
this country before, or at all events about this date,
but they hunted the deer, the hare, and occasionally

the otter, as well as the fox ; warranted perhaps to
hunt anything, from a "hearwig to a helephant,"

We know the first Sir Watkin Wynn was killed
out hunting in 1749, but we are not told with whose
hounds he was hunting, or what was the animal he
was pursuing. The story goes that this Sir
Watkin's second wife, a daughter of Sir Charles
Shakerley, said to have been his own god-daughter,
moreover young and beautiful, dreamed that her
husband was killed out hunting, and begged him
not to go out on that day. He had half promised to
do as she wished, for youth and beauty will have an
influence on us all, when a good-natured friend
intervened, and persuaded him that if he listened to
all the fancies of his wife he would soon have to
give up all his amusements ; his argument prevailed,
Sir Watkin went out, got safely through the run,
but in crossing a field at Acton, near Wrexham (the
seat of Sir Robert Cunliffe), on his return home, his
horse making a peck, pitched him on his head, which
came in contact " with the only stone in the field ; "
and so the dream was fulfilled, for he died on the spot.

This Sir Watkin was celebrated for his Jacobite opinions, which caused him much inconvenience, as in 1745, the year of the young Pretender, he was obliged to leave his home in Wales for a time, to partake of the hospitality of his friend, the Duke of Beaufort, at Badminton. A picture is still, we believe, in existence there of the Duke and the Welsh Baronet looking at a race horse named Grip. A duplicate of this picture was destroyed in the disastrous fire at Wynnstay, on the 6th March, 1858, but the present Duke, with characteristic liberality, again had the picture copied, and presented it to the late Sir Watkin Wynn.

In 1788, another Sir Watkin established a hunt at Wynnstay, which, after being broken up for a time, was revived in 1793, when a dinner and a ball were given at Wynnstay in honour of the occasion; these hounds hunted the hare, except when a bag fox was turned down. The following letter to Mr. Myddelton, of Chirk Castle, from his under agent, shows they occasionally drew for a fox :—

"December 12th, 1793,

"Thursday.

" Hon. Sir,—

"When I got up to the Castle this morning I found a number of horses in the stable belonging to Sir Watkin W. Wynn and two carriages in the yard. On enquiry I found that Sir Watkin and a party of gentlemen were gone out with the hounds to draw the covert near Mr. Walker's, of Glysen, when they found a fox immediately (indeed I find it was Thos. Ganard found him, lying in a "break" of gorse); he ran nearly to the Orsed and back by the slate quarry, and then to the woods by Mr. Walker's, crossed the river above Pont Fadoc, up to Cefn Ucha, and into the plantation. As I was going down the lawn I could hear the pack in full cry and see several horsemen in the plantations. I thought it right to go up there as soon as possible to open the gates, in order to prevent as little damage as possible to the fences, and to assist in getting off the hounds, which was done as soon as the huntsman and whipper-in came up. They had

run the fox very hard, but did not kill him. Thos.
Ganard saw him cross the road into the small plantation facing Hughs' house, but they could not
recover him. I find they had sent to T. Ganard to
stop the earths, but I had not heard it.

" What occasions my troubling you with this letter
is to inform you, Sir, that Sir Watkin enquired
much whether you had any of your horses to dispose of—in particular mares for *breeding*, he was
much in want of. I told him you had a Highflyer
mare and some other young mares that you meant
to dispose of some time back, but whether you had
altered your intentions I could not tell. He begged
I would write to you, Sir, and he desired to know
your answer as soon as I received it. Sir Watkin
admired the mare I had under me (Dod's mare),
and begged to know whether she was to be sold. I
could only tell him that I would immediately con-
sult you, Sir, and that I would let him know as soon
as I received your answer. Sir W. spoke to me
twice on the same subject, and desired that I would
not forget to let him know. If you have anything

to part with, I think this is a good opportunity, and the sooner you determine the better. I heard lately that they are riding the country over for horses for Sir Watkin; he has bought a lot from Mr. Wardle. He asked me if I could tell nearly the price of the Highflyer mare; I could only say that you, Sir, intended having 70 guineas for her some time ago, but I supposed you would not sell her for that sum now. As *Highflyer* was dead, I thought a mare of his get would be now of more value."

In South Shropshire, Mr. Forester, of Willey, hunted an enormous tract of country, while at the same time Mr. Hill, of Prees, and Mr. Roberts, of Wem, kept a pack of hounds, which, we are told, "rarely hunted anything but a fox, though it was generally a bagman." Nevertheless, on the 30th November, 1792, they did find a fox, and a real good one too, in the Twemlows, for he went over a good line of country, and was killed at Tarporley, in Cheshire, after a run of about 60 miles.

The fact, we believe, is that foxes were rather rare animals then. They were not preserved in those days, and neither Beckford nor Somerville (two of the earliest writers on hunting) ever suggested that they should be ; indeed, many old parochial Churchwardens' account-books show that a reward was paid for their destruction, *with other vermin;* and whenever one was seen or heard of, the services of the nearest pack of hounds were called into requisition to hunt him. The fox was then a far hardier and less pampered animal than he is now, living a more frugal life, having to travel long distances in search of the wherewithal to satisfy the cravings of hunger, for, at the time of which we write, pheasant rearing and game preserving in the modern sense, were altogether unknown.

In those days the hunting country of a master of fox hounds was not even confined to a county. The Berkeley Hounds, for instance, hunted from London to Berkeley Castle, in Gloucestershire—a wide stretch of country, but probably not larger than that hunted by the then Lord Yarborough, which covered the whole of the extensive county of Lincoln.

In the *Sporting Magazine* of 1800 there is a list given of all the packs of fox hounds then kept in England; those named are the Dukes of Rutland and Beaufort, Lords Yarborough, Spencer, Berkeley, FitzWilliam, Scarborough, Stamford and Warrington, Sir Richard Puleston, Messrs. Meynell, Corbet, Forester, Warde, Childe, Lambton, Pryntz and Heron, the last being probably the Cheshire Hounds, as George Heron was Master of those hounds about that time.

This list, however, does not embrace all the fox hounds then in England, as we find from hound lists in our possession that, without doubt, Lord Sefton had a pack, and Lord Monson at this time hunted the Burton Country, which he took in 1781.

But besides these there were other packs which hunted the fox, though unknown beyond their own district, probably trencher fed, good hunting hounds, though possibly not very fast, nevertheless showing a great deal of sport to the Squires and Yeomen in their drab breeches and *very* brown top boots, which were duly taken down from their accustomed hook on the "house place" ceiling when they were wanted to be worn in the chase.

Many years ago we were introduced to a pack of these trencher fed hounds in South Shropshire, and the sight of them took us back in fancy something like a century, but fox hounds they were without any doubt, and though perhaps scarcely fast enough for a vale country, they would run and hunt on over those hills as long as anyone would stay out with them, and we were told they accounted for a good many foxes.

Let us now turn to the records of fox hunting in Cheshire. The Tarporley Hunt Club we find was established in 1762, and the rules of this Club give us an insight into the state of hunting in that country at this period. One rule of the Club was "That any member who kept hounds should be invited to bring them to Tarporley for the first week in November, but if no member of the Club kept hounds, then they should borrow a pack and that they should be kept at the expense of the Club during the week." The third rule of the Club shows us the nature of their sport; it runs thus :—" The *harriers* shall not wait for any member after eight o'clock in the morning."

At first the uniform of the Tarporley Hunt Club was a blue frock coat with plain yellow metal buttons, scarlet velvet cape and double-breasted scarlet flannel waistcoat, the coat sleeves to be cut and turned up; a scarlet saddle cloth bound singly with blue, and the front of the bridle lapt with scarlet. A change of uniform in 1769 indicated that *then* the Club had taken to fox hunting; at the same time the number of "collar toasts" was reduced from three to one, except, as the rule directs " when a fox is killed above ground, when another shall be drunk." The uniform then was a red coat unbound, with a small frock sleeve, a green velvet cape and a green waistcoat, the saddle cloth to be bound with green instead of blue; much indeed as it is now, and as described by the Cheshire Poet,—

> " Their coats were red as carrots,
> Their collars green as grass,
> Their spurs were made of silver,
> And their buttons made of brass."

In 1779 Mr. Smith Barry established a pack of fox hounds in Cheshire, which he kept entirely at his own expense, but in consequence of some hunting dispute with the neighbouring landowners, Sir Peter Warburton set up a pack of fox hounds in 1784, which were known as the Cheshire Hounds.

It was, we believe, the same Mr. Smith Barry who matched his celebrated hound Bluecap and a bitch named Wanton to run against Mr. Meynell's Richmond and another, over the Beacon Course at Newmarket, for 500 Guineas. Mr. Smith Barry's hounds were trained at Tiptree Heath, Essex, by the well-known huntsman, William Crane ; their training was to run a fox drag three times a week over grass for eight or nine miles ; they were kept to this exercise from the 1st August to the 28th September, being fed on oatmeal and sheeps' trotters. On the 30th September the match was run by making the accustomed drag from the Rubbing House to the starting post of the Beacon Course, the four hounds being immediately laid on the scent. Mr. Barry's Bluecap came in first,

Wanton close behind second; the Beacon Course was run in a few seconds more than eight minutes, about the same time as an ordinary Plate horse will take to do the course in, with eight stone on his back, and within which time the celebrated horse Eclipse is said to have done the same distance at York with twelve stone up. In this match Mr. Meynell's Richmond was beaten by upwards of 100 yards, while his partner did not run the course through. Sixty horsemen started with the hounds, of whom Cooper, Mr. Barry's huntsman, was first at the ending post, having "rode" the mare that carried him quite blind. Twelve horses out of sixty came in with the hounds, William Crane, mounted on a King's Plate horse named Rob, being the twelfth. The odds of 7 to 4 were laid before starting on Mr. Meynell's hounds, which had been fed on legs of mutton during their training.

This match is very interesting to us as showing the pace hounds could go even before the close of the last century.

About this time Squire Leche, of Carden, had a

CARDEN.

pack of fox hounds with which he hunted his own
side of Cheshire, including the Bickerton Hills,
dipping a good bit into the Vale of Chester, but as it
was his invariable custom to return home for dinner,
as Nimrod relates, and the hour thereof being three
o'clock, we can readily understand that this arrangement would not accord with the convenience of all
who hunted with the Carden Pack; wherefore,
though he went home at his usual dinner hour, he
left his hounds to finish the day's sport under the
charge of "Sam," his whipper-in.

Mr. Leche hunted his own hounds, and it is
recorded that on one occasion, probably after a good
run, "Sam" returned to Carden, having refreshed
himself *not* wisely but too well. The Squire, having
often before this had occasion to complain, said to
"Sam" that he could stand this no longer, but
would look out for another whipper-in, on which the
said "Sam" retorted, "It would be as well for the
hounds if you would look out for *another huntsman*
at the same time." This probably was the only time
that Squire Leche was ever *stopped*, as he was

celebrated far and wide for his clever witty sayings ; needless to say, " Sam " continued in his post as whipper-in, and Squire Leche showed that he could good humouredly *take* what he could so freely *give*.

We are unable to learn the exact year in which Mr. Leche commenced fox hunting ; we know he was born in 1734, and died in 1817, and we believe he kept his hounds on until 1812.

There is now at Carden a curious old silver horn, given to Squire Leche in 1797 by Sir Watkin Williams Wynn, probably not only from the affection and regard of the donor, but in memory of the sport he had shown in the hunting field.

Mr. Egerton Warburton quotes, in his book, a letter from John Glegg, of Withington, showing the sport the Cheshire Hounds had in consequence of Mr. Leche giving the hill foxes a " shaking up " so frequently, recounting a run in 1805, from Baddiley, through Cholmondeley and Edge, to the Shocklach Meadows, where Reynard crossed the river Dee and saved his brush. It must have been a fine run, over a really grand country —distance about eighteen miles.

EMRAL.

In 1817 Mr. Leche died, full of years and in the esteem of all his neighbours. Many a good story have we heard of him from the late Viscount Dungannon and others, which memory refuses to recall.

While he was hunting the Carden side of Cheshire, his friend and neighbour, Sir Richard Puleston, established a pack of fox hounds to hunt the Welsh and Shropshire sides of Emral. When Sir Richard came of age in 1786, he built new kennels on the Hanmer side of Emral Park ; the feeding house is now alone standing, the rest of the building having been pulled down in 1857.

Sir Richard's country was not sufficiently stocked with foxes to allow him to hunt it three or four days a week, so, in addition to his home district, he hunted a great portion of what was then called the Shiffnal and the Albrighton country, having his kennels and stables at Ivetsy Bank, where the hounds and horses remained for two or three months, with an occasional stay of five nights at Newport. His meets in that country were " Red Deer Park," " Chillington," " Donnington Woods,"

"Enville," "Dudmaston," "The Black Hill," "The Lizard," "Aqualate," "Sheriff's Holes," "The Old Lodge," "Stourton Pool," "Rudge," "Wrottesley," &c. There he seems to have shown a great deal of sport, as witness a run from Hilton Park, when his hounds found a good fox in Essington Wood, which was eventually killed, according to his diary, "by two deer *dogs* belonging to Mr. Anson close upon the hounds in Heyward Park, after a most gallant run of two hours and forty minutes."

Good as this run was, it sinks into insignificance compared to one recorded in the *Sporting Magazine* as having taken place with the Montgomeryshire Hounds, when a brown gelding by Snap is said to have carried the whipper-in through a run of sixty miles without a fall, then carried him home twenty miles, making with the outward journey fully a hundred miles. After all it is the pace that kills, though perhaps there are few horses now that can compass such a feat of endurance as this son of Snap is *said* to have done.

A singularly good run is also recorded by Sir

Richard in his diary, when his hounds ran their fox into Chillington Park, where he swam across the large piece of water there, immediately re-crossed it and was soon killed.

In 1801 Sir Richard took his hounds to Shrewsbury for the Hunt Week, when they met one day at Eaton Mascot, another day at Cross Hill, and a third at Atcham Bridge, which, we believe, remains to this day the Friday " meet " of the Hunt Week. On this occasion they had a severe run to the Wrekin and back to Attingham to ground ; this run, the diary says, " lasted three hours and twenty-five minutes ; much distress among the horses and many falls."

In the same year (1801) these hounds having returned to their kennel at Emral had a good run from a covert near Marchwiel Hall for Gresford, and eventually killed him in Acton Park, after a hunting run of two hours and a quarter. ·

Again a good run is recorded on the 29th December of the same year ; the meet was Penley Green and they found a fox in Mill Wood Coppice, ran to Lea Wood, where he was headed back to Bradenheath, thence to Gredington, on for Halghton Hall and Holly Bush, nearly to the Cottage Gorse, back through the Penley Coverts, and he was killed above the Brook Mill, after a run of three hours with a *good scent*, " strange to say " the diary adds, " this was with a vixen, and allowed to be the best run ever seen in this country."

On the 23rd January following they had another good run from the same covert, going past Welsh-hampton to Petton, where he got to ground in the main earth, after a run of three hours and forty minutes—followed by this remark " a large field and many falls, got home to the kennels at seven o'clock, sat down to dinner at eight, supper at two!! The hounds very fresh the next morning and in high glee on Monday."

It is pleasant to read the master's praise of his hounds: " Torment, Grateful, Dramatist and Frolic brilliant to-day." With all this severe work and the long road journeys the hounds had to take—for besides the kennels at Ivetsy Bank, we read of the hounds being occasionally located at Beckford and Prees for Hawkstone—we shall not be surprised to find that Sir Richard was sometimes short of hounds, and it is recorded of him by Nimrod, that he then borrowed Squire Leche's pack, who on this account called him " My Huntsman Dick." Scarcity of foxes was the probable reason why Mr. Leche lent his hounds to Sir Richard; his country was not a large one, and at his time of life he would not like to go far from home, so the arrangement suited him very well, as he gave his country a rest and at the same time kept his hounds in condition.

Notwithstanding the quantity of cub foxes Sir Richard turned down in various coverts in his country each year, we constantly read in his diary of very long draws without a find, a very different experience, we are pleased to add, from that of 1892, in the same country.

Sir Richard Puleston in his earlier years seems to have "hung" a good deal towards the Shropshire side of the country, probably out of affection and regard for his old friend Mr. Corbet, of Sundorne

Castle, who was by many competent people considered to be the best judge of a fox hound then
living, although Nimrod tells us that he always
bowed to Sir Richard's superior judgment in this
respect; be this as it may, many of Mr. Corbet's
hounds were bred from dogs in the Emral Kennels,
and several there from Mr. Corbet's, especially by
his renowned old dog " Trojan," a name that would
at any Shropshire gathering rouse the enthusiasm of
hunting men.

Sir Richard was far too wise a breeder of hounds
to confine himself to one strain of blood, however
good it might be, we therefore find him using Lord
Vernon's Magnet, Mr. Meynell's Gainsborough and
Splendour, the Cheshire Bruiser, Lord Monson's
Matchem, Lord Sefton's Challenger, and several of
Mr. Forester's. Sir Richard, in his diary, gives
great praise to Mr. Meynell's hounds, speaking of
his Matron Famous, who was, by his Dromo out of
Fashion by Fancy, as of an excellent sort, bred by
Mr. Meynell, got by his Grecian, he by Trueman
out of Graceful, " a bitch brought from Ireland by

me." Sir Richard also bred from Racer by Mr. Meynell's Royster out of Rival, in fact he seems to have been much of the same opinion as the Poet who wrote—

"Talk of horses and hounds and the system of kennel,

Give me Leicestershire nags and the hounds of old Meynell."

Without doubt Mr. Meynell had a system of his own which was most successful. His aim in breeding hounds was, as the *Sporting Magazine* of that day said, to produce the steadiest, wisest, best and handsomest pack in the kingdom; he tried to combine strength with beauty, steadiness with high mettle ; the first qualities he considered were fine noses and stout runners. When the hunting season commenced, his hounds were divided into two packs, the old hounds—three seasons and upwards—formed one, no two year old hound being admitted among them except with a high character ; these hunted the best of the country. The younger hounds and the entry hunted the Woodlands and the unpopular meets. Perhaps we may be allowed to add an account of a run with Mr. Meynell's hounds in 1794, taken from the *Sporting Magazine* of that time, especially as two of the foremost men in it bore names honoured in Cheshire and Shropshire.

"Mr. Meynell's hounds had on Wednesday sennight one of the severest runs from Ashby Pastures ever remembered in this country, the whole was one continued burst of an hour and fifty minutes, without an interval of a single check, notwithstanding the change to a fresh scent after about the first hour. As it was not endways run, the huntsmen and three or four others who had skirted with judgment, came up just after the fox was killed, but the only four people who lay well with the hounds were Messrs. Cholmondeley, Forester, Morant, and Sir Harry Featherstone, and their horses were much distressed at the end. The rest of a very numerous field were completely beat from the first, and never made their appearance at all. The unrivalled superiority of the hounds was as remarkable, in their carrying so fine a head during every part of such a severe run, as it always is during a cold hunting run."

To show that the scarcity of the "raw material" was not confined to Cheshire or Shropshire, we add from the same source, "Mr. Meynell was obliged to take his hounds out of Leicestershire for a great part of the season of 1794, to enable a stock of old foxes to get up again." Mr. Berkeley Craven records that he had himself met the Quorn Hounds at Combe Abbey, near Coventry.

All this, however, is a digression for which we ask to be forgiven, and we return to our own country and Sir Richard Puleston. His favourite hound in his own kennel was Dromo, written in *very large* letters in his hound book ; he was by Gainer out of Darling—Gainer by Mr. Meynell's Stormer out of Lord Monson's Traffic; Darling by Sir Thomas Mostyn's Darter out of his Rally; Darter was by Driver, "the property of Mr. Coke, of Norfolk."

There is at Emral a large headstone to the memory of this famous hound with the inscription :

" Alas, poor Dromo !
Reynard with dread oft heard his awful name.
Died September, 1809."

Sir Richard made a great name for himself in the
hunting world. Nimrod, in an article in the
Quarterly Review of March, 1832, says of him, " he
is celebrated as a judicious breeder of hounds, and
his blood has been highly valued in several of our
best kennels, among which is Lord Cleveland's, to
whom Sir Richard sold a large draft some years
ago." There is a graphic account in the *Sporting
Magazine* of these hounds going to Raby Castle
under the charge of one Robert Williams in 1806 or
1807, where they arrived safely after their long road
journey, Robert riding a mare the Marquis had
bought from Sir Richard, which they called the
Puleston mare, and which was for many years, as
well as Robert Williams, a prominent figure in the
doings of the Raby pack. This mare was by
young Snap, son of Old Hundred House Snap,
which Lord Forester considered the best hunting
blood England ever possessed.

Robert Williams, who " personally conducted " these hounds to Raby Castle, commenced his hunting career as whipper-in to Sir Watkin Wynn's harriers, with whom he lived for several years, from whose service he went to that of Sir Richard Puleston, by whom he was " sold " with the draft hounds and the Snap mare to the Marquis of Cleveland. Bob, as he was familiarly called, was an artist of the first pretension, was as hard as nails, had great nerve and would ride anything over any obstacle, with the result that he had broken three ribs on one side, two on the other, *both* his collar bones, and had been *scalped ;* his description of his fall which led to this catastrophe is certainly *telling,* " he tumbled me down as we were coming away with our fox, and kicked me on the head till all the skin hung over my eyes, and do you know, Sir," he added, " *When I got the doctor I fainted for loss of blood."* The last sentence was given in a tone indicative of surprise, Bob evidently thinking that fainting was the exclusive privilege of the fair sex.

At the close of the season of 1812, we believe

Squire Leche gave up his hounds, and then the
Carden side of the country was added to Sir
Richard Puleston's; and as a consequence of this
arrangement Sir Richard gave up altogether the
Albrighton side. All this country, which now forms
so large and important a part of the Wynnstay
country, he continued to hunt until the end of the
season 1832-3, when he finished with a meet at
Emral, on the 4th April, 1833, a fox hunting career
of more than forty-five years. When he retired he
sold his pack to Lord Radnor to go into the old
Berkshire country. These hounds had an extraordinary propensity of singling out some one hound
which had fallen into disgrace with them and
worrying him; in vain did Sir Richard offer a
reward of £200 to anyone who would suggest a
cure for this. It is said that Will Todd, into whose
charge they went, knew nothing of this propensity,
and the very night they arrived at Kingston Inn
Kennels they commenced their old game; Will got
a bell and rang it so loud and used his whip so
freely that he alarmed the whole neighbourhood.

The next day he kept them in the yard and let their unhappy victim go in and out as he pleased to the lodging house, and in the end they were so frightened at the tinkle of the bell, the rope of which was always at his bed-side, that they would stop their quarrel at the slightest jar of the rope.

These hounds were said to have done very well in the old Berkshire country, and were always spoken of in the most flattering terms, when we hunted with Mr. Morland in our Oxford days some years later.

During Sir Richard Puleston's long career as a master of fox hounds, we cannot learn that he had more than four huntsmen. He seems to have begun with Thomas Crane, a son, we believe, of the celebrated Will Crane, who had hunted the Duke of Wellington's hounds in Spain during the Peninsular War, but we have no record of him except that we know *his* son and *his grandson* were in turn Stewards at Emral, and almost to the present date some of the family were respected tenants on the estate. For a short time it was said he hunted his own pack, whipped in by Jack Bartlett, who was as

E

fine a horseman as they make them. Ned Bate
succeeded him, and when Sir Richard grew tired of
hunting his own hounds, he turned them over to
him, and for thirty years he hunted Sir Richard's
hounds, though not without a break, as he
certainly was Mr. Pelham's huntsman when he had
the Shropshire Hounds. At the end of Mr.
Pelham's mastership, Ned Bate returned to his old
master's service, and ultimately was landlord of the
Emral Arms Inn at Worthenbury, a small village on
the bank of the River Dee, about a mile from Emral,
where Ned had served Sir Richard so faithfully for
many years. Bate died on the 4th March, 1855.
The following lines were written to his memory by
a young friend of ours, who, when on a vist to
Emral, delighted to have a talk with the old huntsman and to hear his legends.

" Amid the ancient fields let the aged huntsman rest,
Among old familiar faces whom in life he loved the best,
And as ye pass his quiet bed, ye need not mourn nor weep,
For after his long day of life, old Ned perforce must sleep.
And should he dream, sweet sounds which were of all to
      him most dear—

The Dee in flood and hounds in chase, make music in his ear ;
And should the hunt come near his grave let youth pause
   in his pride,
In honour of the old man who played his part so well,
Until upon his brave true heart Death's closing curtain
   fell."

Two brothers, Will and Tom Roberts, successively
took old Ned's place as huntsman, when he retired
from active service ; the first named of these was
huntsman when increasing years and infirmity compelled Sir Richard to relinquish the office of M.F.H.,
but as he could not live without hunting in some
shape, for a few years longer, indeed almost to the
last, he kept a pack of harriers.   He died at Emral
in 1840.

Cecil, in his Records of the Chase, says of him,
" Sir Richard Puleston, a very distinguished sportsman, considered the best judge of fox hounds of his
time, hunted divers parts of Shropshire, and indeed
other counties, during a period of between thirty
and forty years ; to point out the various districts
and precise dates would be now impossible.   During
the latter part of the time he confined his hunting to

the neighbourhood of Emral in Flintshire. I never
met his hounds but once, which was at the Twemlows
near Whitchurch, a great many years ago, and have
but a slight recollection of them."

During the time Sir Richard hunted the Shropshire side of the country, a notable affair in the
hunting world occurred. The Woore, belonging to
Mr. Wickstead of Betley, the Shropshire, under the
management of Sir Edward Smythe, Mr. E. M.
Smythe, and Mr. William Lloyd of Aston, and the
Cheshire, under Sir Harry Mainwaring, sent seven
couples of hounds each to a meet at Shavington,
then the seat of Earl Kilmorey, on the 7th April,
1829. It was a trial of speed between the three
packs. Will Head, of the Cheshire, as the senior
pack, was appointed huntsman, while Will Staples,
of the Shropshire, and Wells, of the Staffordshire,
were in attendance. It was a brilliant sight, for not
less than two thousand horsemen made their appearance, of whom seven hundred were in scarlet; and
there were carriages full of ladies without number.
At eleven o'clock the hounds were thrown into the

great wood at Shavington, found a fox immediately, had a fast ringing run for thirty minutes and lost him. They had a scurry with another, which they killed in Lord Combermere's Park. Then came the run of the day; finding a fox in the Sedges by the side of the lake, they went away at a good rate with the hounds well at him in a body and carrying a good head. Flying through the park, they crossed the Chester Road and got somewhat clear of the crowd of horsemen that pressed upon them; the pace served the hounds, and so too did a "regular yawner" that made the leading men swerve from the line to look for a weak place; it was a sunk fence, broad and deep, with stiff rails on the top; the height and the width made it nearly impossible for a horse to clear it in his stride. While they were hesitating at the obstacle, the voice of Jack Mytton was heard saying, " out of the way you fellows, here goes for the honour of Shropshire ; " down came his " Hit or Miss " mare with Mytton under her ; bleeding, hatless and torn, he remounted his mare, which had been brought back to him, and rode bareheaded through the rest of the run. The hounds, with a greatly diminished following, were stopped at the end of an hour, as they were then running a vixen heavy in cub. Will Head, never having left the hounds and as it were first up, was awarded the brush ; Will Staples, of the Shropshire, however, won two sovereigns from Will Head on the wager of whose hounds should first taste blood.

It seems to have been the general opinion that Chaunter, Orator and Ambrose were *the* hounds of the day.

This account is taken from the *Sporting Magazine* of that date, but as we have, through the kindness of Mr. Frank Bibby, of Sansaw, the loan of Will Staple's Diary, we venture to give his version of this day's sport.

" April 7th. Met at Shavington (half-past ten) with seven couple of the Cheshire hounds, seven of Mr. Wicksted's, and seven couple of ours, total twenty-one couple ; drew Shavington Wood, found and went away very quick to the Styche, from there to Cloverley, by the house and the gorse, where we came to a check, and there being a large field the hounds were pressed so that they were *drove* from the scent ; afterwards they hunted a cold scent back to the covers at Shavington. But the gentlemen belonging to the Cheshire were not satisfied, they thought the hunted fox was gone for Combermere. Head made a wide cast on that line, but to no effect. We then went on to Combermere, found by the pool and killed him ; it was thought he was the fox from Shavington, as he had a good chance of getting away, supposed to have been beat. As soon as the hounds had eat him there was a view " halloa " the other side of the pool (by the house). We got away with our fox, and had a very pretty run of twenty-five minutes; when the hounds were running into their fox it was perceived that it was a vixen ; we stopped the hounds. We drew one cover after, but we did not find. We went to Wrenbury, and spent a pleasant night with our fellow sportsmen, and each party steered for their respective homes the next morning. The hounds that were there are as follows :—Auditor, 5 years old, Chaunter, ditto, Folly, ditto, Rarity, 4 years, Jolaz, ditto, Pangloss, ditto, Joker, 2 years old, Joyful, Lucifer, Challenger and Valentine, ditto, Ambrose, Virgin and Workman, 1 year old, Parasol, 5, Bashful, 3, Vanity, 2, Champion, 2, and Ranter 'was' at Wrenbury, but did not work. The horses we rode were Mr. Lloyd's Brian O'Lin and the chestnut mare ; I rode Rowton, Jack, Red Robin. 1 fox."

This, no doubt, is a fair account of this day's sport, and it seems to settle the point that Will Head was huntsman on that occasion.

Sir Richard Puleston, who had gone to Shaving-ton with his hounds to hunt there the next day, reluctantly allowed his whipper-in, young Ned Bate (having refused him once) to have a ride with these 21 couples of hounds, with the result that he killed his master's horse.

Old Ned Bate never tired of talking of this memorable day, but whether he showed any sport or not on the following one, this deponent cannot recollect.

In the season of 1833-34, Sir Rowland Hill

occasionally brought the Shropshire Hounds to the kennels at Emral, and sent his horses to Old Ned Bate's stables at Worthenbury, and hunted from there, Brynypys, Burton's Wood, the Wyches, and a great part of Sir Richard Puleston's country, some of which the Shropshire Hounds continued to hunt for a good many years, but the coverts we have named were, in the season of 1834-35, given up to Mr. Hurleston Leche, of Carden Park, son of the old Squire, who had hunted the Cheshire side of this country for so many years, who had then established a pack of fox hounds with Will Head as huntsman, old Joe Sinclair (who had been hunts-man to his father) as first whipper-in, with Gaff, son of a Cheshire huntsman, second. These were all bred the right way to show sport, and on the few occasions on which we were out with them they certainly did.

Mr. Leche hunted much the same country as his father had done, with the addition of the Emral Coverts, Brynypys, and the Wyches. The Shrop-shire having got possession of Iscoed, Gredington,

F

Bettisfield and Hanmer, continued to meet there, as
Will Staples' diary shows, for some years, besides
drawing Oteley, Petton, Lineal and other places
which seem naturally to belong to the Shropshire
country.

Mr. Leche unfortunately did not live long, and
hunted the country only for six or seven seasons.
When his hunting establishment was broken up, his
son and successor to the estate being only a boy at
the time, his fox hounds were sold in 1841 to Mr.
Price of Brynypys for 500 guineas for the late Sir
Watkin Wynn, who came of age in that year.

Mr. James Attye, who then rented Penley Hall,
was made master of the hounds with a subscription,
a goodly portion of which was paid by Sir Watkin,
who was at that time in the 1st Life Guards. His
military duties detaining him in London or Windsor,
prevented him assuming the command of the hounds,
though he purchased them and found kennels at
Lightwood Green for them.

Mr. Attye was a fine horseman and a good sportsman, and made an excellent temporary substitute for

Sir Watkin. His country included that part of Sir
Richard Puleston's which the Shropshire had re-
tained, as well as all Mr. Leche's country. The
meets of his hounds were Chorlton, Wynnstay,
Gredington, Carden, Pentrebychan, Hardwick,
Gallantry Bank, Bettisfield, Churton, Hampton
Heath, Penley, Gresford, Emral, Brynypys, Shock-
lach, Queen's Head, Burras, Halston, Chirk Castle,
Iscoed, Whittington, Nescliffe, Worthenbury,
Pradoe, Plas Teg.

Mr. Attye made Will Grice, who had been first
whipper-in to the renowned Will Staples, his huntsman, and Will Smith, who had been huntsman to
Mr. Leche, whipper-in. We have no record of the
sport Mr. Attye showed during the two seasons he
was master, but we have a pleasant memory of some
good gallops with him ; especially of one from a
small covert at the King's Mills, near Wrexham, to
Burras Wood, going first nearly to Holt, racing all
the way ; and another from Grafton Gorse passing
through Barton to Holywell Gorse.

In the year 1842 Sir Watkin Wynn bought the

Perthshire Hounds from Mr. Grant, eldest brother of
the celebrated artist, Sir Francis Grant, and sent
them to Lightwood Green kennels to join those he
had bought when Mr. Leche died.

At the end of two seasons Mr. Attye, as we have
said, retired, and well do we remember being in
Birmingham when his horses were sold there, two of
them being bought by Mr. Fitz Hugh, of Plas
Power, and brought back into the country, one of
them a grey horse whose name we have forgotten,
the other a brown horse named Jailer, who invariably carried his new master right to the front.
After Mr. Attye gave up the hounds he left this
country and went to live in Rugby, where we have
had many pleasant evenings with him, and he would
speak with much pleasure of his hunting experiences
in this country, and would talk of Burton's Wood
and other coverts in it as if they were personal
friends.   Unhappily he has years since "joined the
majority," but his memory will live long in the
hearts of his many old Rugby friends.

CHAPTER II.

"Of a fine old English gentleman
Who lived on his estate."

Now we come to the bright era of the mastership of Sir Watkin Wynn, and it seems only fitting that we should tell something of his antecedents. He was born in London in 1820 (a good vintage year) educated at Westminster, from whence he went for a short time to a private tutor to prepare for Oxford, where he entered Christ Church College in October 1837; there he remained for two years, but academical studies did not *quite* suit his taste, as they interfered too much with the pursuit of the fox; so he gladly took his leave of Alma Mater in July, 1839, to join the 1st Life Guards as a cornet. Four years' service in H.M. Household Cavalry quite satisfied him, so in 1843 he shaved off his moustache, then only worn by cavalry officers; the badge of slavery he called it, and went in for the far more

congenial office of M. F. H., and the duties of the
owner of large estates.

Long before Sir Watkin left the Life Guards—
indeed we believe as soon as he came of age—he
had been elected M.P. for his native county, Denbighshire, which he continued to represent without
interruption to the day of his death.

Early in his career, Sir Watkin had been made a
Member of the Jockey Club, and as long as he was
in the Life Guards he always had a few horses in
training under the care of William Scott, but as far
as our memory carries us, not after he left the Army,
hunting being more to his taste than racing. But
incredible as it may seem to those who in later
days knew Sir Watkin's figure and weight, we once
saw him ride a race in his own colours, red and
green, at Gorhambury Park on his horse Remnant,
against his brother officer, Lord Glamis (afterwards
Lord Strathmore) also riding his own horse Sedi-ben-
Sedi, which we are pleased to add the Welsh
Baronet won, possibly from following his trainer's
advice not to ride in spurs or carry a whip.

This, we believe, was the only occasion on which Sir Watkin sported silk, and soon after this he parted with his small racing stud.

Even when in the 1st Life Guards, young as he was, few men were better known in London among all classes than Sir Watkin Wynn, for whether he was "tooling" his splendid team of browns from Knightsbridge Barracks, or driving his cabriolet along the streets with perhaps the best stepping gray horse in London, or riding his hack in Rotten Row, his figure was at once spotted almost as much as it was in after years, when he rode his dun brown mare, followed by Jonathan Phillips, the neatest of grooms and the most faithful of followers, one who for more than twenty years rode second horse for Sir Watkin, and who was nearly as well known as his master, both in London and in the country, and we think it only fair to add, no man was ever more respected in his walk in life than Jonathan Phillips.

In 1843, Sir Watkin having left the Army, assumed the management of his own hounds and became the head of fox-hunting in this part of

England. With a princely establishment, with the
very best horses England or Ireland of that day
could produce for love or money ; hounds improving
every year ; youth, wealth, health, and a strong love
within him of the noble science, he began his
successful career as a master of fox hounds. Sir
Watkin was by no means a feather weight, but
the horses he managed to get together with the aid
of Major Cotton, McGrane, of Dublin—that Anak
of horse dealers, as he was aptly named—and John
Darby, of Rugby, seemed to carry him almost without an effort. He invariably bought young horses,
which were usually ridden quietly about by Simpson,
his stud groom, and then when they had had two
years' Wynnstay oats and hay in them, *if found good
enough*, they generally carried their master for some
years. Sir Watkin had a strong seat, a light hand,
good nerve, and a quick eye to hounds ; he never
pulled his horses mouths about, and therefore though
he *courted* one very often, by galloping down all
sorts of lanes, and cramming his horses through
blind places, he seldom had a fall, and never we

believe a serious one. His horses in his early days
were always *well-bred,* never less than sixteen hands,
with the very best of shoulders, legs and feet. Sir
Watkin seldom or ever " flew " a fence, but trained
his horses to jump the widest ditches and even the
Grafton and Aldersey brooks at a stand, to creep
through a thick blind fence with a big ditch on the
other side; then when he dropped his hand, his
horse jumped, and immediately he scuttled away as
fast as the horse could gallop; thus he got over the
country amazingly, and has puzzled and surprised
many a young one who followed him to see what
places his horses carried him through or over,
apparently with the greatest ease. A remarkable
instance of this occurred on December 23rd, 1863,
when his hounds found at Sandford Pool, near West
Felton, a good fox that ran over the bogs and then
took a good line up to Porthwain lime rocks, where
he was killed after a fast forty minutes. Colonel
Lloyd and another got over the bog somehow and
saw the run. Sir Watkin jumped a drain fully four
yards wide, and by galloping down a road got up in

G

time to see the fox killed.   Usually Sir Watkin rode
the same horse all day until the hounds turned their
heads towards Wynnstay kennels.

When Sir Watkin took over the management of
his hounds, his meets were much the same as those
of Mr. Attye, with slight additions; it was not till
the season of 1847-48 that we find him meeting at
Hawkstone, Styche and Cloverley, owing to their
hunting arrangements in Shropshire falling through;
this was great luck for him, as it gave him an
addition of some of the finest parts of Shropshire;
and all the country which had been taken by the
Shropshire on the retirement of Sir Richard
Puleston, and which had not been given up to
Mr. Attye, was now given to him, including Petton,
Halston, Woodhouse and Aston, thus he hunted
the cream of Shropshire, a very fine part of the
Chester Vale, including Aldersey and Carden, both
sides of the River Dee from Wynnstay to Eaton
Hall, and practically, all the country lying between
Wynnstay and Whitchurch, and beyond this Sand-
ford, Cloverley, Shavington and Styche.

Sir Watkin having built kennels near the Park Eyton entrance to Wynnstay, removed his hounds to them very soon after the commencement of the season of 1845, the horses then as now being stabled at Wynnstay, except some eight or nine kennel hacks. At this time there were some 55 couples of hounds in the kennels, and from fifty to sixty horses in the stables at Wynnstay, a truly princely establishment, and coming, as Sir Watkin did, from the schooling of the first regiment in H.M. Service, as we should expect, the servants' liveries, saddles, bridles and appointments were of the very neatest. At this time he lived in what he was pleased to call a Cottage, near New Bridge, about a mile from the stables at Wynnstay ; there he stayed for some three or four years, and returned there after Wynnstay was burnt down.

Sir Watkin continued Will Grice in his service as huntsman, and though at this time we have no record of the doings of the Wynnstay Pack, we have a distinct recollection that there was a great increase in the number of foxes in the country, and we have no doubt that everything possible was done to show sport.

Mr. Myddelton Biddulph sends me an account of a run from Erbistock Wood, during Grice's last year, to Eaton Hall, where they killed their fox in the garden, after a very fast run, and over a good country, past Borras—a ten mile point. Only some three or four saw the finish, including Lord Rane-lagh, who was riding a horse of Col. Myddelton Biddulph's, of Chirk Castle, where he was staying, Miss Humphreys, and Will Grice.

In 1847 Will Grice died, and Sir Watkin promoted Jack Woodcock, who had been first whipper-in, to be his huntsman. Unfortunately he was not a success, possibly because he lacked *head;* we remember he was a neat horseman, was very quick in turning hounds, but a *good deal* more than this is necessary to make a huntsman. So in the following season he left Wynnstay kennels, and by a lucky turn of the wheel, was succeeded by " merry " John Walker, so deservedly looked up to by all fox hunters of his day. Sir Watkin was most fortu-

nate in securing his services, as it was said Lord
Suffield offered him 500 guineas a year to go with
him into Lincolnshire. Walker had been "farming"
the Fife Hounds, some of which he brought with
him to Wynnstay, the rest of the pack having been
sold to Sir Richard Sutton, he had them sent by train
from Scotland, met them at the nearest station, and
threw them at once into a gorse covert, where they
found a fox, and gave Sir Richard one of the best
runs he ever had in Leicestershire.

These hounds had been very carefully bred for
many years, and there was some of the purest fox
hound blood in England in the kennel. We have
before us a list of these Fife Hounds in 1828, and
among them we note :—Bustard, by Lord Darlington's Bustard ; Novelty, by Lord Kintore's Nestor ;
Remus, by Mr. Osbaldeston's Comet; Trident, by
Mr. Osbaldeston's Pilot ; Duchess, by Sir Richard
Puleston's Trojan ; and four couples by Sir Richard
Puleston's Dasher.

Besides some few of his hounds, Walker brought
with him two or three horses which Sir Watkin had

bought from him ; one of these was a dark chestnut horse named Nimrod, well known to the writer of this ; he had not particularly good shoulders, and was generally considered far better in the hunting field than he was afterwards at the stud.

We gain some insight into the history of John Walker from the *Sporting Magazine*, which tells us " When Mr. Grant gave up the Perthshire Hounds, which Sir Watkin bought, there were a good many sportsmen there who were most unwilling to give up the amusement of fox hunting ; they therefore made an arrangement with Walker to bring the Fife Hounds into Perthshire and to give them six weeks' hunting in the year, three weeks in November and three in March." The *Sporting Magazine* of 1843 gives an account of his arrival at Moncrief kennels with thirty-six couples of hounds and fifteen " nags," all in high condition ; the writer says "the Fife Hounds had all the requisites of a first rate pack of hounds, the dogs ranging about 24 inches and the ladies nearly up to the same standard, all very level, strong and powerful on their legs." "Of the qualities of John Walker, as he is familiarly termed by his intimates, the best eulogy is that he has hunted these hounds eighteen seasons in his little Kingdom of Fife, and according to the opinions of those who have followed him, he knows how to draw a covert and find his fox handsomely ; that he is quick and bold in the field ; that he possesses those invaluable qualities in a huntsman, patience and perseverance ; that no man enjoys a run more than he does when hounds settle to their fox ; that he is just as happy to kill him in the woodland as in the open ; that his eye is perfect to hounds ; that his casts are made with a rapidity everyone must admire ; that none can beat him in a straight line over a difficult country. In a word his heart and soul are in the chase, and his nerve and judgment surpassed by few. Of his steeds it is only necessary to say, his fifteen hunters are the right stamp for a difficult or, indeed, any country."

We have transcribed the above for the simple reason that we believe it to be true, and in our judgment John Walker fully bore out in this country the reputation he brought with him from Fifeshire, for no man could have shown better sport than he did when he was huntsman to Sir Watkin Wynn's hounds; or have taken more pains in the improvement of the pack. His quickness in getting away with his fox was apparent to all who hunted with him, and his perseverance was shown by his sticking to his fox until he could either *handle* him or mark him to ground.

Walker was not celebrated for suavity of manner, but his good sense and tact prevented him from needlessly offending anyone who was hunting with him, though we know well that his temper was often *stretched;* never perhaps more so than when he warned a stranger not to ride over his hounds, and was told "well take your hounds out of the way." Happily this sort of thing did not occur every hunting day, and it was generally enough for Walker to hold up his hand when he saw his hounds were pressed upon by a large and eager crowd and say, " Hold hard, gentlemen, I *pray* you do." Usually this was followed by the hounds hitting off the line.

when he galloped away, saying in a stage whisper, "That will do, *now* ride over them."

It was universally allowed here, as in Scotland, that as a huntsman, Walker was of the *best*; quick in his judgment, his eye always *going* to see which hounds were hunting the line and where they had brought it to; and then his nerve was so good, his seat, for a short legged man, so strong, and his hands so light, that he never *stopped* his horses, and no fence, large though it might be, ever *stopped* him, therefore, however long and severe the run, he seldom mounted his second horse till his master said, " Go home, Walker, we will not draw again." Then no doubt he felt the advantage of having a fresh horse to carry him back to Wynnstay kennels, often a precious long way off, as the said kennels are placed on the "outside edge" of the country. Well do we remember on one occasion Walker running his fox to ground in a rabbit hole near Edge Hall when Sir Watkin told him to take his hounds away, which he reluctantly did; out bolted the fox, and in vain did the hounds run him almost to Peckforton Castle,

H

when it became so dark they had to be stopped,
though the fox was viewed before them dead beaten.
A long ride we had before us through pitiless rain,
Sir Watkin's brougham having been sent to
Worthenbury. Walker and his hounds had fully
twenty miles to jog before they reached Wynnstay
kennels.

Walker was especially fortunate in having two
such good *aides* as George Wells and Trueman
Tuff, both of whom well deserve all the praise we
can give them. And very excellent sport was the
consequence of this able management. Mr.
Boughey, a very old and respected follower of
these hounds, sends us an account of a run at this
time from Loppington to the Wrekin ; the *longest*
in his forty-five years' experience. He adds also an
amusing incident of a fox running into the town of
Whitchurch and there hiding himself in a cesspool,
but in vain, as Sir Watkin gave one of Messrs.
Smith's men from the foundry a gratuity (which he
richly deserved) to pull him out, which he did with a
pair of tongs.

The following runs, sent us by Mr. Myddelton Biddulph and Mr. Edmund Peel, two distinguished sportsmen in Sir Watkin's country, are well worthy of preservation :—

" Ran from Rednal Gorse, past Sandford Pool, crossed the Severn and Vernieu without a check to the Breidden Hill—nine mile point, but about 13 as the hounds ran, 1 hr. 10 min. Only three really saw the run, Colonel Lloyd, of Aston, Colonel Cotton, and Trueman Tuff, second whip."

" January 11th, 1858.—Met at Macefen, found a fox in Clutton's Gorse, ran to Lowcross, where we lost him. Then found in Large's Gorse a fox which ran as if going to Broughton Gorse, but turning to the left crossed the Malpas road between Cherry Hill and Malpas, through the Wyche Brook near Dymock's Mill; keeping the Wyches well on the left hand, we arrived at Iscoed, skirting the Park, crossed the Whitchurch road and on towards the Fenns, which we left on our right, over Whixall Moss, and killed him at Fenn's Bank, after a run of two hours and a half. About fifteen saw the finish, among whom was Mrs. Clement Hill, who went capitally on Ganymede. Walker was delighted with the run, and regretted the absence, at the finish, of Sir Watkin, Colonel Cotton and Mr. White, who were obliged to leave at the Wyches. I had my second fall of the season at the last fence."

It was on the 6th March in this year, 1858, that the calamity happened which caused this country to be hunted as a subscription pack for a second time ; the first being the two years when Mr. James Attye was master ; now again this occurs owing to the disastrous fire at Wynnstay, when the mansion and most of its contents were destroyed. The hounds were to have met on that day at Broughton Hall. After a long " wait," a whipper-in came over bearing the sad news. Strange to say, though Wynnstay is not more than three quarters of a mile from the kennels, the mansion and its contents were nearly all destroyed before the men at the kennels heard of the fire ; the reason probably of this was that a fierce hurricane blew all through the night, which drowned every other sound a hundred yards

off. It was a fearful sight we saw when we reached
Wynnstay; the whole neighbourhood seemed to be
collected in front of the burning ruins on the lake
side of the house, labourers, colliers and friends
huddled together in one confused mass, the gale
blowing the sparks of fire high into the air, and
many engines playing on the ruins apparently
without the slightest effect. The only source of
comfort amid this fearful disaster was that though
the house was full of servants and visitors, there
was no loss of life or personal injury to anyone.
Among those who were staying at Wynnstay at the
time, and who lost very valuable diamonds and
jewels were Colonel and Mrs. Cotton, and Lord and
Lady Londonderry. The loss of works of art
belonging to Wynnstay was simply irreparable;
fortunately however some of the "Sir Joshua's"
and "Wilson's" were saved from destruction, having
been sent to London at that time to be cleaned.
Sir Watkin and Lady Williams Wynn bore their
misfortune with a bravery that could not be excelled, and most cordially did their neighbours, and

indeed the whole of North Wales, sympathise with
them, addresses of condolence literally pouring in
upon them from all quarters of the Principality.

Sir Watkin having no residence from which he
could hunt the country, decided to go abroad for
the winter, and for that season relinquished the
management of the hounds, which Colonel Cotton
took over, with a subscription, a very liberal
portion of which, however, came from Sir Watkin,
who moreover lent his hounds and kennels and the
stables at James' Farm, Ruabon, where his hunters
were always summered.

On the 8th May we find this entry in our diary:
—" Went to the Wynnstay sale of Sir Watkin's
hunters ; a great many people there." There were
indeed very many there from all parts of England,
the day chosen for the sale being the Saturday in
Chester Race Week.

The horses were eagerly competed for, and
probably realised the highest average of any stud of
hunters at a sale in England under the auctioneer's
hammer up to that date. They were brought out

looking wonderfully well, and in perfect condition, and reflected the greatest credit on Simpson, Sir Watkin's stud groom. It was universally admitted that a better looking lot of weight carrying hunters were never brought out of one stable, or horses with better legs and feet. It was thought by some that "Constantine" was the pick of the basket, though in consequence of a report that he was a roarer, he was sold for a considerably less sum than he ought to have been, and his purchaser could have had a hundred pounds for his bargain before the end of the sale.

"King Dan" was greatly admired; he was a rare instance of a hunter who could carry eighteen stone or ten stone, with equal ease to horse and rider. Mr. Anderson, of Piccadilly, took him, as he also did "Cassio," intending to keep the latter for his own riding, but horsedealers are ever open to a "deal," and we believe he passed him on to the Marquis of Ailsa. Cassio was said to have been out of a 15 hands mare by Income.

Phœbe was brought out looking more like a five years' old than a mare who had carried Walker for eight seasons; she had not a scratch or a blemish about her, and we scarcely know whether we ought to give the credit of this to the mare or her rider. Walker certainly should have a share, as during his first ten years he only killed one horse for his master.

This was a sad day for Simpson, the stud groom, as he saw favourite after favourite knocked down under Mr. Tattersall's relentless hammer without reserve. Simpson, we may add, was quite a household name at Wynnstay; from the time he left the box of the Devonport Mail no one's figure was better known in the neighbourhood of Wynnstay than that of Henry Simpson, whether he was riding the blue pony over Wynnstay Park to James's Farm, or schooling one of Sir Watkin's young ones; he seemed equally at home and could not be mistaken. He, too, is gone; the light of his life went out of him when he lost his master.

The following is a complete list of Sir Watkin's horses sold on the 8th May with the names of the purchasers :—

			£	s.
1.	Allen - - -	Anderson - - -	52	10
2.	Captain Copp -	Ditto - - - -	86	2
3.	Bay harness horse	Croft - - - -	84	0
4.	Brown ditto -	Grunly- - - -	46	4
5.	Brown ditto -	Anderson - - -	86	2
6.	Brown ditto -	Fletcher - - -	60	18
7.	Whitelegs - -	Finnie - - - -	89	5
8.	The Cob - -	Darby . - - -	110	5
9.	Railway King -	Anderson - - -	115	10
10.	Black hack- -	Darby - - - -	105	0
11.	Chestnut ditto -	Fletcher - - -	89	5
12.	Grey gelding -	Darby - - - -	38	17
13.	Forester - -	Hill - - - -	84	0
14. 15.	} Driven together -	Sir H. de Trafford	} 126 95	0 11
16.	Crosby - -	Pilgrim - - -	173	11
17.	Judy - - -	Darby - - - -	63	0
18.	Black mare- -	Lambton - - -	63	0
19.	Orlando - -	Croome - - -	141	0
20.	Touchstone -	Percival - - -	73	10
21.	Young Nimrod -	Ditto - - - -	55	13
22.	Twemlows - -	Robinson - - -	96	12
23.	Morella - -	Bailey - - - -	59	17
24.	Constantine -	Broughton - - -	183	15
25.	King Dan - -	Anderson - - -	483	15

I

						£	s.
26.	Turk - -	-	Percival	-	-	- 262	10
27.	Brown gelding	-	Milne -	-	-	- 131	5
28.	Cymbeline -	-	Darby -	-	-	- 120	15
29.	Phœbe	-	Kenyon	-	-	- 50	8
30.	Kathleen	-	Thornhill	-	-	- 80	17
31.	Capsule	-	Croome	-	-	- 77	14
32.	Cromaboo -	-	Darby -	-	-	- 315	0
33.	Balloon	-	Milne -	-	-	- 173	5
34.	Cassio	-	Anderson	-	-	- 651	0
35.	Judge -	-	Lloyd -	-	-	- 173	5
36.	Castor	-	Gillmour	-	-	- 283	10
37.	Dunshangton	-	Percival	-	-	- 84	0
38.	Bay gelding	-	Darby	-	-	- 210	0
39.	Pongo	-	Ditto -	-	-	. - 210	0

On the whole the sale was most successful, as in those days the hunting public were not educated to give sensational prices. All, we believe, that were put up were disposed of; some few horses were withheld from the sale, so Simpson's office was not quite a sinecure; but it was not until the spring of 1859 that the stalls in Wynnstay stables were once more filled and Simpson seen as of yore, distributing oats among his equine friends, or sitting on

HENRY SIMPSON.

a coffer in Wynnstay stable eating some himself, while he expatiated on the merits of the various "quads" under his eye.

CHAPTER III.

"Give me the man to whom nought comes amiss
  One horse or another, that country or this,
Who through falls and bad starts, undauntedly still
  Rides up to the motto—' Be with them I will.' "

EGERTON WARBURTON.

We now come to the year of office of Colonel
Cotton as master of the Wynnstay Pack; a most
successful one it was, perhaps the best hunting
season Walker had in this country. This was the
result of its being a specially good scenting one,
indeed the hounds seldom went out during the
whole of it without having a good run; added to
this, Colonel Cotton and Walker pulled together
with the greatest harmony, they were both thorough
sportsmen, and each worked with "a will" to show
the country all the sport they possibly could; and,
as we have already said, they succeeded in their
object. We shall, however, only give one or two as

COLONEL COTTON.

specimens; one of which was on the 10th January, 1859, and is thus described by a friend (Mr. Edmund Peel):—" Met at Gredington, where we found a fox, but soon lost him; then another went away through Gredington, leaving Bettisfield on the right of us as if for the Fenns, turned to the left by Iscoed, and killed him at Tushingham. A splendid run; hounds getting away from Walker, Hassall, and Rowland Hill, the only men who got a start. I saw nothing of this run." This must have been a very fine run.

Mr. Myddelton Biddulph tells of another in January, 1859, when they ran from Clutton's Gorse, and killed their fox in the open, just before reaching Cholmondeley. Then drew Rawhead, ran fast from there across the best of Cheshire, without touching any covert except Spurstow, killed in a farmyard at the Bache House, beyond Hurlestone. Fifty minutes.

It was during Colonel Cotton's mastership of these hounds that Bangor Hunt Steeple Chases were inaugurated, the first meeting taking place there on the 25th February, 1859. The origin of the meeting was a sporting match across country, between the Hon. Lloyd Kenyon and the present Richard Myddelton Biddulph, then a cornet in the 1st Life Guards, which Biddulph won. It was then suggested that they might as well make a day of it, have a farmers' and a gentlemen's hunt race, and this proved so great a success and was so popular among all classes, that the meeting has been continued to the present day. The next day out hunting Walker had a very severe fall near the Gerwyn, and, as our diary says, was taken home in our carriage by a friend who had gone to the meet with us, which, we believe, was at Cock Bank Gate. Fortunately, however, there were no bones broken, so in a few days' time Walker was once more in the hunting field.

At the end of this season, on the 7th May, 1859, Colonel Cotton's horses were sold by Messrs. Tattersall, to whom we are much indebted for their kindness in sending us the details of this sale, which we give.—His forty-eight horses realized 5,900 guineas ; the following twenty-five, 100 guineas or more :—

					Guineas
Cornelian -	-	-	Lloyd	- -	120
Coquette -	-	-	Darby -	- -	130
Captain	-	-	Lord Dacre -	-	140
Cloe -	-	-	Robinson	- -	190
Columbine	-	-	Sir W. W. Wynn-	170
Charity Boy	-	-	Siburn -	- -	155
Citadel	-	-	Hunt -	- -	160
Caliban	-	-	Sir W. W. Wynn-	170
Cheese Cake	-	-	Ditto -	- -	240
Cheese Monger-	-	Brooke-	- -	125
Coningham	-	-	Sir W. W. Wynn-	115
Walls Eye-	-	-	Darby -	- -	130
Cato -	-	-	Bateman	- -	135
Cricket	-	-	Lord Ossulston	-	165
Chance	-	-	Lord Forrester	-	215
Prince of Orange	-	Drake -	- -	210
Colwich	-	-	Darby -	- -	220
Creole	-	-	Shakerley	-	125
Folly-	-	-	Crawford	-	330
Cinderella-	-	-	Devenport -	-	205
Carlisle	-	-	Denison	- -	290
Cockatoo -	-	-	Darby -	- -	290
Coronet	-	-	De Winton -	-	305
Cannock -	-	-	Crawford	-	305
Caution	-	-	Garth -	- -	115

We note in our diary, 7th May, 1859. "Drove
Capel Croome to Cotton's horse sale, and on to
Ruabon. Cotton, Frank Dawson, Lloyd Kenyon
and Robinson called on their return from Ruabon.
All, alas, gone from us."

This sale bears strong testimony to the good
judgment Colonel Cotton displayed in selecting
high-class hunters; and on two other occasions
when Messrs. Tattersall sold at Combermere
Abbey, his stud of horses brought equally high
prices, the result of the first sale being 5,904
guineas, and on the second, in 1871, sixty-two lots
produced 8,891 guineas.

No man in England or Ireland was better fitted
to be a M.F.H. than Colonel Cotton; he was a true
lover of sport, it seemed to matter but little to him
whether it was fox hunting, racing or shooting,
indeed he did not look down upon hare hunting,
and for some years kept a pack of harriers, and
when spring came he was equally ready to go out
with the otter hounds. Into all and each of these
sports, in their turn, he threw his whole soul, and

appeared to be as much interested in it as if it was
his favourite pursuit. His manners were most
genial at all times, and were especially cordial in the
hunting field, where he had a kindly greeting for
everyone he met, in whatever station of life he
might be, with a *slight* preference for a *tenant*
farmer ; this made him especially popular, indeed it
would scarcely be too much to say, beloved by all
who knew him. Then his keenness in everything
relating to a horse or a hound, was most refreshing ;
no hour was too early for him to begin hunting,
no distance was too far for him to go for a " hunt,"
and he was always willing to draw for a fox, as long
as any daylight was left, or anyone would remain
with him.

The *horse* certainly came first with him in the
dumb animal world, and he spared neither money,
time or trouble in buying the best he could find in
England or Ireland. Across the Irish Channel he
was quite as well known as he was in Cheshire,
never missing Punchestown or the Dublin " show,"
and perhaps no private gentleman ever bought in

K

Ireland and brought over to England so many high-class horses as he did. As a judge of weight-carrying hunters he was unsurpassed, and his services as a judge of them were eagerly sought in England and Ireland ; he never seemed more in his element than he was with a lot of good young horses before him in the show ring.

For many years Colonel Cotton was M.P. for Carrickfergus, but his heart was not in the "business," and so little did he trouble St. Stephens, that the doorkeeper of the ladies' gallery there, once told a friend of ours "I can tell you the name of any member you like, madam, I know them all *except* the Hon. Col. Cotton, member for Carrickfergus." It is possible that his knowledge of members of the House may afterwards have been extended, as Colonel Cotton was for a brief period Parliamentary Secretary to the Master of the Ordnance or in some similar post, and therefore was obliged to be in the House of Commons when Parliament was sitting.

Gladly did Colonel Cotton relinquish the trammels

of office for pursuits more congenial to his taste amid the pastures of Cheshire.

Colonel Cotton was born in Barbadoes in 1818, his father being Commander of the Forces and Governor-General of the West Indies at that time. Lord Combermere had greatly distinguished himself in India and in the Peninsular War, and was commonly known as the Cheshire Hero. The great Duke of Wellington was a personal friend of his, and sponsor to his son, who was named Wellington after him—Wellington Henry Stapleton Cotton, afterwards better known in the 1st Life Guards as "Cheese," was educated at Eton, and was also at the same private tutor with Sir Watkin Wynn, where their life-long friendship was formed. Wellington Cotton matriculated at Oxford, but was "scratched" for his University engagements in 1837, and joined the 7th Hussars in Canada, where he soon distinguished himself as a sportsman not only with his fishing rod among the salmon in the Canadian rivers, but as the best shot with a gun in the British Dominion there, and a most successful steeplechase rider. After being in Canada for some time with the 7th Hussars, he was appointed to the 1st Life Guards, of which regiment his father, Field-Marshal Lord Combermere, was Colonel; here again he was associated with his old friend, Sir Watkin Wynn, besides many other congenial spirits, among whom were Lord Glamis, Sir Charles Kent, Lord William Beresford, Sir Hervey Bruce, Sir Richard Sutton, Colonel Bulkeley, and many others, who were well known in the hunting and sporting world.

In 1846 Wellington Cotton got his troop, four years later, in 1850, his majority, and was made a Colonel in 1857.

Even in his early years, when quartered at Windsor, Wellington Cotton showed a decided love of agriculture, and would do a little cattle and sheep feeding, for which purpose he annually bought a field or two of "Swedes"; this taste was afterwards much developed, and he became well known as a feeder of cattle and a breeder of Berkshire pigs, some of which he occasionally exhibited at the "Royal."

In connection with Berkshire pigs we once witnessed an amusing scene at the Birmingham Cattle Show, whither we went with Colonel Cotton and Sir Watkin. Wellington Cotton had persuaded Sir Watkin to let him try and buy for him a Berkshire boar which was exhibited there; the owner demurred to the price offered and suggested that Sir Watkin should give more for him, on which the Colonel said, he was sure he would not give a *farthing* more, and that the owner had better take the price offered or there would be no sale, adding, " Sir Watkin is a *confounded pig-headed Welshman,*" the said Sir Watkin standing a few feet away, smothering his laughter by cramming his pocket handkerchief into his mouth.

Under the tuition of John Walker, Wellington Cotton soon became almost as good a judge of a fox hound as he was of a hunter, and was as well known at the annual Hound Show at Peterborough as he was at the Agricultural Hall at Islington Horse Show.

Colonel Cotton also took great interest in the

breeding of thoroughbred stock, and though not an
owner of either brood mares or sires, it was mainly
through his interest as a large shareholder and
director that Stockwell and Newminster, the well
known horses, were purchased by the Rawcliffe
Farm Stud Company, both of whom were so
eminently successful at the stud.

During the time Colonel Cotton was master of
the Wynnstay Hounds he resided at Cherry Hill,
situated near Malpas, about nine miles from the
kennels, but probably about the centre of the
country they hunted. There he continued to live,
until the death of his father, Field-Marshal Lord
Combermere, when his duties as owner of one of
Cheshire's fairest seats caused him to remove to
Combermere Abbey, to the great regret of all his
neighbours.

To the end of his life Wellington Cotton, second
Viscount Combermere, was a man of extraordinary
energy and "go," it seemed to make but little
difference at what hour he went to bed or got up in
the morning, his usual order to his servant was "call

me at six o'clock," unless he happened to be going from home and then he would name four or five o'clock. Wherever he went, to Ireland, Scotland, Canada, or the West Indies, he was always on the "rampage," as if he had not an instant to lose ; he would rush off to see the latest improvement in some agricultural implement, an exhibition of sporting pictures, or " Buffalo Bill," and failing any of these, he would go to see anyone's horses that were to be sold ; friend Horace's words were ever a true description of his character " Cœlum non animam mutant qui trans mare currunt." The best of neighbours, the warmest of friends, the most generous and popular of landlords, was the united verdict of all Cheshire when he passed away. Always hospitable, ever considerate, generous almost to a fault, what wonder that he was deeply regretted when he fell a victim to a cab accident one dark winter's evening, when coming from Herkomer's studio, where he had been sitting for the finishing touches to his portrait, which was being painted for the members of the Tarpoley Hunt Club—which we are told is a most accurate likeness, and we trust it will serve to keep green the memory of one to whom Cheshire was so dear—one who was ever seen at the " Swan," as if he was the youngest and most cheery of the members of the club :—

> " At Tarpoley glorious
> Always uproarious
> Combermere Abbey young man."

The distress that was felt throughout this neighbourhood at his unfortunate accident may be readily imagined, though no one for a moment feared for his life. He himself described the accident in a letter to us, as having happened through a hansom cab coming suddenly on him from behind a cart, the cab horse cutting into him "like an over-reach in a horse." When he rushed forward to get out of the way he ruptured all the muscles above his knees. He was apparently getting over the accident fairly well, and had, as he described it, "taken a canter on crutches," when the want of his usual exercise told upon him and threw his heart out of gear, and he died very suddenly at his rooms in St. James's Place, on 1st December, 1891. Greatly were we shocked by receiving a letter from him and another from his son Richard put into our hands at the same moment, the one written in fairly good spirits, the other announcing his father's death.

" Dear Mr. Puleston,—You will be shocked to hear of the sudden death of my poor father; a clot of blood was the cause ; he was only ill half-an-hour. " Sincerely yours,

" R. S. COTTON."

Never was a larger gathering of mourning friends than when he was buried in the family vault in Wrenbury Church by the side of his honoured father, whose funeral we also attended, joining Sir Watkin Wynn at the Holly Bush Gate and going with him to Combermere Abbey.

There was, as we should expect, more show at the funeral of a Field-Marshal of England and a Colonel of the 1st Life Guards, with his charger bearing his helmet, and some of his troopers following, besides all the tenantry on horseback ; but we

L

feel sure there could not have been more genuine
sorrow than there was when Wellington Henry
Stapleton, second Viscount Combermere, was laid to
rest in the presence of so many old and valued
friends ; among whom were both the masters of the
Cheshire Hounds, Mr. Corbet and Mr. Park Yates,
Sir W. W. Wynn, Mr. Oakeley, Mr. Heywood
Lonsdale, Lord Enniskillen, Colonel Rivers
Bulkeley, Lord Kenyon, Lord Trevor, Mr. Peel, of
Brynypys, Mr. Godsal, of Iscoed Park, Mr. Leche,
of Carden Park, Mr. Cudworth Poole, with very
many other leading gentry and tradesmen of the
district.

Gladly we turn from this sad scene to the renewed
mastership of Sir Watkin Wynn.

CHAPTER IV.

"Come, unkennel your hounds, let's away to the field,
   For the morning is charming and gay,
   To hunting all pleasures and pastimes must yield,
   To fox-hunting all must give way."

OLD HUNTING SONG.

When the hunting season of 1859-60 commenced, Sir Watkin and his staff seemed once again to resume their accustomed places in the hunting field as if there had been no interregnum. From the diary of a friend (Major Thoyts), who hunted with the hounds at this time, we add the following notes of the sport Sir Watkin and his hounds showed, to carry on the history of the country. "25th January, 1861, the meet was at Carden, but the run of the day was from Royalty Covert, whence the hounds followed their fox nearly in a straight line past Castletown Gorse, leaving Shocklach on the left hand, across the Worthenbury Meadows to the Cottage Gorse, where they changed foxes, and ran to Brynypys."

On 21st March in this year our friend's diary tells of a fox being chased and killed by a single hound.

On the 23rd January, 1863, he writes: "A three o'clock! fox was found in Sutton Green Covert, which ran by Llwynknotia and Cefn to Marchwiel Gorse, then by the Parkey and Bowling Bank to near Ridley Wood, and was killed in Jones' Farmyard."

"31st January, 1863. Ran from Peel's Gorse to Duckington, where they killed their fox in an hour (about a thirteen mile point); the hounds were sent home then, though it was not much after one o'clock, but they had run directly away from the country that was stopped."

Again, "4th February, 1863. They had a rare day's sport, running their first fox from Royalty to Saighton, where they lost him; found again in Tom Iron's, and killed him at Beeston Castle, after as fine a run and over as good a country as any man could desire to ride over." Col. Lloyd had the best of this run. This and the one from Royalty to Brynypys Walker talked about for years.

John Walker in the Carden Valf.

19th February, 1863. A capital run from Mace-fen ; killed in the Shocklach Meadows. The Duc d'Aumale was out, and went well for a part of this run.

7th March. Forty minutes from Holywell Gorse, by Aldersey and Tattenhall, nearly to Saighton.

Then we find a run from Macefen Gorse, past Malpas and Edge, ultimately killing their fox on the Broxton Hills, after a run of an hour and twenty-four minutes.

3rd December. Met at Sarn Bridge. Found directly in the Wyches ; ran for Stockton, where he turned to the right hand for Emral, and on nearly to Penley, back once more to the Wyches, then to Burton's Wood, but they were obliged to give him up, as the shades of evening were upon them, though he had been viewed only just able to crawl a short time before.

17th March. They had a good run from Petton over the meadows past Loppington, and bearing to the right, killed on the top of Grinsell Hill, one hour twenty minutes. We believe that Myddelton

Biddulph and Jack Jones went very well in this run.

There is also another good run described from the Wyches, which we give as a finale with Walker, when they killed their fox in the open at Wallington, after a good hunting run of two hours and ten minutes. The fox was evidently making for the main earth in the Cottage Gorse, which, however, he had not strength to reach, though only four fields off.

We have said a good deal of the *sport* Sir Watkin's hounds showed when Walker and Payne carried the horn, but hitherto have told nothing of the hilarity and fun we had in the hunting-field, and the good-fellowship and kindly feeling promoted by joining in the same sport, which was not confined to one class, but shared by all "the field." There always appeared to be some chaff going on—a dirty coat to raise a smile (there is something in the misfortunes of our best friends that is pleasing to us), or as in the sketch before us, certain friends trying, in vain, to get their horses over a brook, while others are *in* it.

A Scene at Aldersey Brook, 1865.

Some legend to be told which the Baronet brought fresh from town probably that morning by the Irish mail, and, as we have already said, the good-fellowship seemed so general as to cause a Leicestershire friend whom we had mounted to remark, " I never saw such a jolly field as yours ; you all seem like brothers," and so sometimes we were, but *" in adversity,"* when we could not get over a brook, or in the not unknown experience of when we had lost the hounds.

These are about average "specimens" of the sport Walker showed Sir Watkin and the country, until gout and *Anno Domini* compelled him, in 1865, to relinquish the arduous and responsible duties of hunting a pack of fox hounds four days a week.

When Walker retired from active service after his eighteen years at Wynnstay, the love of hunting did not die within him ; indeed, he appeared to take as much interest in the sport as when he carried the "horn," and was constantly seen at the covert side even at meets very wide of his new home at Marchwiel. His old friends Lord Combermere and

the Hon. Edward Kenyon, of Macefen, and, indeed,
many others, being ready to give him a mount whenever he wanted one.

As we have said, the foundation of Sir Watkin's
pack of hounds was Mr. Leche's, to these were
added Mr. Grant's, and, in 1845, five couples of
hounds which Sir Watkin bought at the sale of Mr.
Foljambe's hounds for 500 guineas. With these
materials and the few Walker had brought with him
from the Fife, he soon got a good pack of hounds
together by the judicious use of Belvoir Royal,
Champion, Gainer, Sultan and Comus, Lord
Yarborough's Chaser, Orator and Harper, Lord
Henry Bentinck's Contest and Craftsman, and
Fitzwilliam's Singer.

In 1855 a litter was entered by the said Singer
out of Rarity, a daughter of Brocklesby Rally-
wood and Mr. Foljambe's Sparkler. One of these
was Royal, Walker's favourite hound ; and a right
good-looking dog he was. When old Tom Sebright
came to Wynnstay to see the entry, and learning he
was by Singer, whom he thought the staunchest

JOHN WALKER ON "SHROPSHIRE."

and best hound ever bred at Milton, he did not want a second look at him before giving Walker the emphatic assurance, " You have got a plum."

From a list of the Wynnstay Hounds before us of 1859, which we obtained when we went with Colonel Cotton to see the entry, we find there were then fifty-five couples of hounds in the kennels, including that year's entry of fourteen couples. This list shows how largely Walker bred from the Belvoir, which he considered the best fox hound blood in England ; there we find Annatole, by the Duke of Rutland's Champion, Pagan by his Royal, Gaylass by his Gainer, Clara by his Lucifer, Reveller by his Foiler, Primrose and Prudence by his Guider. Walker also bred from Sir Richard Sutton's Trueman and Saucebox ; Sir Tatton Sykes' Champion ; Lord Henry Bentinck's Champion and Craftsman ; Lord Fitzwilliam's Marmion, Boaster, Hardwick and Singer ; Lord Yarborough's Rockwood, Pleader and Harper ; Mr. Foljambe's Sparkler. This was indeed going in for all the best fox hound blood in England, and it certainly repaid the cost, which was

M

doubtless considerable, as the hounds were soon as "sightly on the flags" as they were undoubtedly good in the hunting-field.

Walker's favourite Royal will long be remembered, as we have his likeness in the picture by Sir Francis Grant, of Sir Watkin and Lady Williams Wynn; he was a handsome light coloured hound, a painstaking worker, with good legs and feet and a rare nose; this enabled him to lead the pack for nine seasons and to hunt with them eleven; yet, perhaps, in the opinion of many persons well qualified to judge, he was not an unmixed good, as Walker used him far too freely, though undoubtedly he got some excellent hounds—one especially, Statesman out of Stately; for a more useful, sensible hound than he was never hunted a fox.

Poor old Royal was allowed to roam about the Wynnstay kennels to the end of his days.

CHAPTER V.

" Such a pack of hounds, and such a set of men,
   'Tis a mere chance if ever you see their like again."

—OLD SONG.

Before we pass on to the further history of the
Wynnstay Hounds, we should like to say something
of those who distinguished themselves in the field,
and of that far larger body of gentlemen who,
though seldom seen in the front rank in a fast run,
rarely missed a day's hunting, and probably enjoyed
their day's sport quite as much as those who were
resolved to be first, come what might.

Memories crowd quickly on our brain when we
wish to write of them, and the great difficulty is
with whom to begin, so we take first four green
collar men, members of the Tarporley Hunt, though
constantly seen with Sir Watkin's hounds in our
early youth, when the meet was on the Cheshire
side.

Sir Richard Brooke, of Norton Priory, a very
neat quiet horseman, *always with hounds*; John
Glegg, of Withington, with powerful seat and ready
hand; and Harry Brooke, of whom the poet
wrote—

"Quite out of sight of those in the rear."

But the hardest of them all, good over any country,
rough or smooth, was John White—for some
years, till, we believe, 1855, the master of the
Cheshire Hounds; however, even then he managed
to squeeze in a day with Sir Watkin something like
once a week, when the meets suited. Like the
other three green collars whom we have named, he
was always close to the hounds when they ran.

No man of his day was better known in the
sporting world than he was; he was sometimes
called Leicestershire White, Black White, Captain
White, or Jack White, but under each of these
names he was equally well known, and everyone
knew who was meant. Captain White was born in
1790, and was educated at Eton and Oxford (what
a name he would leave behind him at the dear old

Varsity). After he had taken his degree in 1811, he studied "the noble science" under the "Old Squire" (Osbaldeston) at Lincoln. That country however, was scarcely good enough for him, so he migrated to Melton in 1815, where he was a conspicuous figure in the hunting field for a great many years. Hunting was the chief business of his life, though he did not object to throw in a little racing in the summer. Whether he was specially successful on the turf or not, it is not our province to decide, but without doubt he reached the top of the tree as a fox hunter, and probably would have done the same had his taste led him to choose the Army or Navy as a profession; for his indomitable courage, perseverance, coolness, energy and disregard of danger would have made him anywhere what the Cheshire Poet called him, "That Great Commander." In very truth he did command his large Cheshire field; his deep powerful voice, his keen black eye, and shaggy brow made the young men of Manchester and Liverpool shake in their saddles and obey.

"Says he, 'Young men of Manchester and Liverpool, draw
    near,
I've just a word, a warning word, to whisper in your ear;
When starting from the cover side, ye see bowd Reynard
    bust,
Ye can have no hunting if the Gemmen go it fust.'"

. Verily John White was "sui generis" in the
hunting-field, albeit he took very good care not to
spoil his nerve by either eating or drinking anything
that would upset it, and he told this deponent that
he had thrown under the table of the old Club
House at Melton hundreds of glasses of as fine
Bordeaux as ever was landed in England, when a
bumper toast was proposed, so that he might be at
his best the next morning at the Covert side. At
seventy-five years of age, he was as active and
vigorous as many a young man of whom he was old
enough to be the grandfather, yet he "succumbed"
after a short illness from eating a mutton pie, in the
same year as Osbaldeston, the year of the Rinderpest in England, 1866.

We doubt very much whether the youngest among
us will see his like again, for whether he was riding

over the Leicestershire pastures or the Cheshire
Vale, he would take no denial, he would be there.
So, too, would his old opponent Lord Wilton.
Many a tussle had they together in silk and scarlet,
on the race course and in the hunting-field. Lord
Wilton was only occasionally seen with Sir Watkin's
hounds on the Cheshire side, when he was staying
at Eaton with his brother, the Marquis of Westminster; it was indeed a treat to see him go to
hounds, his bright black eye marked out his line,
and despite any ordinary obstacle, he took it. Like
all the Grosvenors we have known, he rode like a
sportsman and looked like a thorough gentleman.
Lord Wilton, too, was one of the most accomplished
and successful gentlemen riders of his day, always
being on Touchstone when he was allowed to do so.
Perhaps his best race was when, riding Chancellor,
he defeated Osbaldeston on Catherina.

There were also other well-known members of the
Tarpoley Club who were constantly seen with these
hounds when the meet was Aldersey or Carden :
" Jemmy " Tomkinson and Bolton Littledale, the

" backbone " of fox-hunting in Cheshire, the best of
sportsmen, the kindest of friends, and the most
popular man in the hunting-field in Cheshire of his
day ; Cecil de Trafford, with his placid, pleasant face,
ever determined to be in the front rank ; and with
him we would couple his brother Augustus, both
very bad to " beat," as also were Reginald Corbet,
the present master of the Cheshire Park ,Yates,
Henry Tollemache and Frank Massey.

For some years we also constantly saw amongst
us Lord Macclesfield ; for his weight of the very
highest class.   He was ever ready to run down by
the Great Western, have a gallop with Sir Watkin's
hounds and rush back again in the evening to hunt
his own pack in South Oxfordshire the next day.
He too came sometimes from Eaton, as well as from
Macefen and Wynnstay, and this reminds us that so
far we have not mentioned the Duke of Westminster, for a number of years, until 1866, we
believe, master of the Cheshire Hounds; he ever
rides *right to the front*, and moreover it is recorded
of him, in the veritable pages of " Baily," that in

company with three kindred spirits, he swam his horse over the river Dee in flood, and stopped the rest of the field.

So far all the men we have mentioned, except the Duke of Westminster, were not residents in this country, but there were then as now, many men who did live in the Wynnstay Hunt, who took their part in a run, no matter who was out; Henry and Robert Clive to wit, both of whom hailed from Styche, and before *their* time even, Charles Eyton, very quick, but a *little* jealous. Of him the story is told that when hounds were running to a brook a friend suggested to him that there was a ford close at hand. " So much the better," he said, " but my horse has seen the brook, and will be very uncomfortable all day unless I let him jump it, so here goes ! " Then there was Bowen of Coton, William Hassell of Bubney, and his brother " Tom," Henry Crane (always in the van), Thomas Lloyd Fitzhugh, invincible, on the Jailer or his little brown mare, when he *quite* liked the country, Richard Lloyd of Aston, with a quick eye to see a fox and with

N

courage to pursue him. His Honour Edward
Kenyon of Macefen, as good a sportsman and as
true a friend as ever broke bread, one who in the
hunting-field and everywhere else, always went quite
straight.

Of Sir Watkin Wynn, our master, we have
already said that he had an extraordinary knack of
getting over a country, the great feature of which
was that he could *gallop*, and no mistake, so that at
the slightest check he would be up and immediately
ask "where did they bring it to ; " this, however,
sometimes was rather overmuch for Walker, and he
would trot on, saying, "Beg yer pardon, Sir Watkin,"
and if his cast was lucky, gallop away. If they
were breaking up the fox he would invariably ask
"What do you want?" Walker generally answered
by "Only a couple, Sir Watkin."

Like other people, Sir Watkin had favourites
among his horses, and he would always be near his
hounds when riding those who had gained his confidence, to wit, Jerry Abershaw, Cromaboo, Comet,
Locomotive, Venus, Cassio and others. Considering

the weight he rode, he certainly struggled on in a run in a wonderful way, and *never ceased galloping until he saw the finish.*

During about the whole of Walker's administration John Drake, of Malpas, was a constant attendant in the hunting-field; he was "own" brother to the Squire Drake and Uncle to the Tom Drake, who were so well known and deservedly popular in this country in after years. The chaff of the family was that John could only go well on a pony, but we never saw anything of this, and if he only had his *own whip and spurs,* and somebody else's horse, *provided it was good enough,* he always seemed most difficult to shake off, and when he was riding his own horse, the "Student," the same might be said. By the way, he sold the "Student" to Dicky Biddulph, which, he said, made him a horseman, which was probably quite true. Then, like a meteor would come among us in November or the end of the season, Sir Roger Palmer, of Cefn, who was seen at his best on his chestnut mare, or "Onyx," though he always rode good horses and went well on them.

At this time, too, Edmund Peel, of Brynypys, was always in the front on the Crow, the Gipsy, and a host of others, as neat as he is determined, sometimes, too, in a silk jacket, William Owen, of Woodhouse, a real lover of hunting *and* a fox, Lloyd Kenyon of Gredington, now most worthily represented by his only son, the present Lord Kenyon, who is himself quite A 1 across country. Lloyd Kenyon was ever "full of ride," and not afraid of embracing mother Earth, which he consistently did whenever he went out fox-hunting. Jack Jones, of Mossfields, is, we are happy to add, still with us, and as pleased as ever to ride *first* over the most cramped country in the hunt.

Then we must not pass over Lord Richard Grosvenor, John and William Coupland, Pierce Hope, to whom the loss of an arm seemed to make no difference in his ability to get to hounds ; Major Barnston, Colonel Barnston, Clayton, Dumville Lees, George Barbour, McGregor, Robert Parker, Horatio Behrens, with his brothers Julius and Frank, Wilding Jones, and most certainly not Phillip

Godsal, with ready joke and genial laugh, always eager to enjoy the sport and to the utmost of his ability to promote it by finding "the" animal, nor John Leche, of Carden, and Tom Aldersey, of Aldersey, both formerly Green Collar Men, and equal to find a fox at any time in their coverts, and certainly in Walker's day to ride after him; the same may with equal truth be said of Sandford, of Sandford, his brother-in-law, Cudworth Poole, and Robert Ethelston, of Hinton; the Honourable Henry Gore often came among us, and later on his "big brother" George (always to the front), Charles Mostyn Owen, Aymer Lane, the Honourable Cecil Parker, Frank Whitmore, Alfred Darby, Robinson, William and Philip Gill, Percy Cross; then we add the names of the two Rasbothams, both neat and accomplished horsemen, the father dating from the time of Mr. Hurleston Leche, and hunting continuously in this Country almost to the present day. A contemporary of his was Colonel Boates, of Rosehill, whose portrait is given in the Wynnstay Hunt picture. The Colonel had been with his regiment, the Blues, at the Battle of Waterloo, and his old Colonel, Sir Robert Hill, used to tell how "Billy" Boates (his name was Henry), when his charger was shot under him, asked to have a trooper's given up to him, which, however, Sir Robert refused, as he believed in his fine tall men, and told "Billy" to go to the rear, but it is said he soon re-appeared, having caught a horse on the field. We mention this legend because the Colonel always showed the same pluck in the hunting as he did on the battle-field. The likenesses of Branker, of Erbistock Hall; Campbell, who made Campbell's Gorse, and left it to Sir Watkin; Tom Oswell, of Ellesmere, and Salisbury Mainwaring (as a boy) all appear in the Wynnstay Hunt picture, and they were habitually seen in the hunting-field, as also were Major Thoyts, who then lived at Pickhill Hall, Ryder of Ellesmere, "Bucky" Owen, of Tedsmore, Peter Bentley, of Westfelton, Carstairs Jones, of Hartsheath, and Henry Bailey, of Gerwyn Fawr. Edmund Swetenham, of Cam-yr-Allen, and Simon York, of Erddig, Longueville, of Llanforda, and Stanley Leighton; all these were "good men and true" and devoted lovers of the chase.

A notice of Sir Watkin Wynn's field in Walker's day would be very incomplete without the mention of two black Squires, both well known in this neighbourhood; the first of these we name was Edward Dymock, of Penley Hall, who also figures in the Wynnstay Hunt picture; the most hospitable of country gentlemen and a thorough fox preserver; his care indeed extended to every living thing which came under his roof—once indeed to a fox which sought shelter in Penley Hall, where he was safely locked up until the hounds returned to Wynnstay kennels, when poor pug was released from durance— we hope to come to an honourable end some other day, when Sir Watkin's hounds met at Penley Hall, which, by the way, was always the place of meeting on the opening day of regular hunting. Dymock was universally popular, always kind to everyone with whom he came in contact, to the poor who wanted it, as well as to the rich who didn't: one peculiar foible he had, however, which we mention with reluctance—most certainly not to cause pain or hurt anyone's feelings—this was a love of the marvellous, which, however, always took a most amusing form, and was, we believe, the sole object he had in view. One day he described a man as having jumped into a well when out hunting. "But how did they get him and his horse up again?" was asked; when he replied with the gravest of faces, "They pumped him up." On another occasion, when showing a lady the old Moated Garden at Penley Hall, he described how the house that stood there was besieged in Cromwell's time, when the "defendants" drove off their assailants by pelting them with *handfuls of bees*, taken from the hives there! These, and the account he gave of the hares sitting on the gate posts in the Worthenbury Meadows in the time of a flood, are fair samples of this amusing weakness. We are much pleased to balance this by saying that no one ever heard Dymock repeat an unkind thing of anyone, or knew him do an ungenerous action; and sad was the day for Penley when he was buried in that churchyard.

We had then also another black Squire, Lloyd Wynne, of Nerquis Hall; he seemed to look upon it as a duty to go out hunting, and punctually he fulfilled it. Born and bred in the country, one of the Fletchers, of Gwernhaylod (he took the name of Wynne), he knew everyone and everyone knew him, and having hunted from his boyhood with Sir Richard Puleston's hounds, knew every covert and lane in the country, and where a fox was going, sometimes better than the fox; he too was universally popular, and being a bachelor was usually staying in someone's country house; so much was this his habit, that a jocular friend once said of him, "most people *keep* a horse, but Lloyd Wynne's horse keeps him." Many good stories are told of him, none perhaps better than that of his going with friends to stay at some hotel in Liverpool for the Chases, when, at the conclusion of his visit, some mystic figures were presented to him known to some as the "reckoning." Among the items on this slip of paper was "apts, £2 2s.," which he thought an

o

imposition, saying "Apples, I never had any!" This naturally caused much amusement to his friends, who jokingly told him the charge was made because they thought he was a lord—they did mistake the name of Lloyd Wynne for Lord Wynne.

His unbounded good nature and pleasant manners made him welcome at the house of every yeoman or squire, and it was a part of his religion to cultivate brotherly kindness by making a call on someone on his return from hunting, and have a chat and possibly a glass of beer.

In the reign of Walker and Charles Payne there was always a Brassey of Cuddington, a Vernon of Tushingham, and certainly in the latter's time Johnson of Tybroughton, who seems equally pleased to follow his beagles on foot as Sir Watkin's hounds on a good horse, though we think the same could scarcely be said of Weaver of Castletown.

All these whom we have named formed generally the "field" with Sir Watkin's hounds in Walker's time; the field, however, then was very different in numbers to what it now is; many a time have we been out hunting and seen only some twenty or thirty men out, the extension of railways accounting probably for the large increase.

In later days came Colonel Rivers Bulkeley, whose superior in the hunting-field and *between the flags* we have never seen ; Frank Cotton, of whom much the same may be said ; Lord Chesham, so aptly described by Lady Alexander Paget as a "nailer to hounds young man"; Lord Cholmondeley, who can both gallop and jump; Archie Peel, whom nothing can stop ; Richard Myddelton Biddulph of Chirk Castle, who has never forgotten the lesson the Student taught him, and who seems to have inherited the riding qualities of his father and mother ; Lord Alexander Paget and his brother Berkeley, quite of the best ; Lord Enniskillen, Henry and Edward Thurlow, James Smith Barry, Sir Robert Cunliffe, the two Ormrods, the two Lovetts, Jack of Fernhill, and Heaton of Belmont, the latter of whom especially seemed happy when riding "Charlie"; Menzies and Sanbach, straight and good ; and another of the Malpas division, Parsons, to whom we must add

Heywood Lonsdale, who knows more of woodcraft than anyone we are acquainted with, a knowledge that he daily (Sundays excepted) puts in practice; his son, Henry Lonsdale (very hard), Arthur Lloyd of Leaton Knolls, always seen to advantage on a certain grey horse ; Lord Hill, than whom we have never seen a man whom a dog loved more, or who could ride a horse straighter across country; the latter may be said of his cousin, Clement Hill "from the Shropshire," who still thrusts right to the front ; to these we must add in conclusion Edmund Bridgman and Frank Bibby, of whose hospitality perhaps we know more than of his horsemanship, but if equally good, it is of the best. Thus much we can answer for, that no man in Shropshire has worked harder than he has done to keep fox-hunting going therein ; and it is to this county (Salop) that all the last six persons mentioned belong, except Heywood Lonsdale, whom we claim as one of us, for he resides in the country and owns large possessions in it, and has for many seasons hunted in this country.

We should like also to say something of the

" visitants " who arrived as regularly as the wood-
cocks, our old friend Granville Somerset being
perhaps the oldest of these in point of the time he
first appeared among us, his genial polished manners
ever insured him a hearty welcome, as year by year
he visited his old Westminster chum, Sir Watkin, as
also did Rowly Conwy, Willie Wynne, Charles
Williams, and in later days, Herbert and Bobbie
Wynn, all from Wynnstay. Of course, there were
many others constantly at Wynnstay, as Sir Watkin
was as hospitable a man as ever lived, even in
Wales, and that is saying as much for him as we
know how to put it ; but they were only *casuals*.
Then in Charles Payne's day, George Best constantly came from Iscoed, and Arthur Brocklehurst
from Cholmondeley Castle, whose brilliant horsemanship demands, though it needs it not, all the
praise we can give it.

But, without doubt, the best known of these was
Squire Drake, one of Sir Watkin's greatest friends,
who, though never a resident in the country, was a
large owner of property and fox coverts in it, and—
needless to say of a Drake—a staunch fox preserver.

From time to time he came to Wynnstay, and far more frequently when he found he could do something for his friend by cheering him up when his health was failing, and when he saw him fairly well he would thoroughly enjoy a ride over his own acres, or anybody else's for the matter of that; and though he would talk of seeing all his host of children in every ditch he jumped over, no one could beat him when riding Gogglehead or Secretary from Castletown Gorse, which Sir Watkin always drew when " the Squire " came to Wynnstay. Tom Drake was born in 1818, the same year as Combermere, and eventually succeeded his father as Master of the Bicester Hounds, and continued to hunt them until about 1863. After this time he had more leisure to come into this country, where his large stock of legends, boundless good humour and love of chaff made him ever welcome. Alas! he, too, is gone from us, but to the end of his life he maintained the high character which the Drakes of Shardeloes have ever held in Cheshire, as sportsmen, landowners and country gentlemen.

But before we pass from the gentlemen who composed Sir Watkin's field to the ladies, we must add the names of those of the military who were best known among us, hailing from the depôt centre at Wrexham. General Mostyn, Colonel Williamson, Charles Mostyn Owen (a resident now in the country), Captain Robert Ethelston, and Captain Fenwick, of whom the same may be said, and Fred Cowan (as straight after a fox as he is on a pheasant). These, and indeed many others, ever formed a very pleasant and cheery addition to Sir Watkin's field, and one and all took their part in a good run.

Many others there were whose names do not recur to us, but we should not like to omit Charles Thorneycroft, Wynne Price, Cartwright Enery, —with an exasperating name—Philip Beattie (ever to the front) and Llewellyn Parry his successor in the same hunting box near Hanmer. Then, as a matter of course, there have always been some professional men whose love of sport caused them to take their well-deserved recreation in the hunting field. Among these were a few black coats, John

William and Henry Armitstead, three brothers all
well known with us and in the Cheshire field, none
of whom could truly say, as the curate is reported to
have done to the Bishop of Oxford, who rebuked
him for going out *fox*-hunting—" Well, my Lord, I
have heard of you at a ball " to which " Soapy Sam "
answered, " I am seldom in the same room with the
dancers," to which the unblushing curate said with
splendid audacity, " and *I* am seldom in the same
field with the hounds ! ! ! " " Bob " Trower and
" little " Cox might be bracketted with them. Of
the latter a good story and a *true* one was told.
When a certain gentleman was out pheasant shooting
with Sir Watkin, the guns were told not to shoot
hens in a particular covert, which the " certain "
gentleman did not hear, and when Sir Watkin
passed him, he cautioned him not to shoot Cox, who
had been sent forward. At the end Sir Watkin asked
" Who shot all those hens ?" to which our friend,
rather pleased with himself, replied, " I did, Sir
Watkin ! " The Baronet said : " I told you not to
shoot hens." " No, Sir Watkin, you told me not to

shoot Cox "—which raised a chorus of laughter from the "guns" at the natural mistake. Then there was Mr. Etches, of Whitchurch, who delighted in a good horse ; but especially worthy of record are two members of the medical profession, who, though well able to take their part in a good run, were ever ready at the call of duty to give up their day's amusement in the case of an accident and attend to the sufferer. These were Dr. Lloyd, of Chirk, well known in the Badminton County before he came among us, and Dr. Jordison, of Malpas.

But even in the earliest hunting times we can remember the gentlemen did not always have hounds to themselves when the scent was good and the pace fast ; they had the ladies to reckon with when a good fox was found, and this, we must not forget, was before the third crutch was invented. Among these, Mrs. Clement Hill, perhaps, deserves the pride of place. Her name has already been mentioned as going so well on Ganymede in a run from Large's Gorse ; for years she seldom missed a day's hunting, probably from the beginning of

P

Walker's reign to the end of Charles Payne's.   Her
sister too, Mrs. Paulet Somerset, was constantly
seen out with us; they were daughters of Jack
Mytton and therefore bound to ride.   These, with
Mrs. Myddelton Biddulph, of Chirk Castle, and her
cousin Miss Humphreys, and Miss Palmer, of Cefn,
were about all the ladies who hunted in this country
when Sir Watkin took it.   They were all well turned
out with the neatest fitting habits the " Poole " of
that day could make, and mounted on the best
"quads " that money and judgment could procure.

Quietly they took their places when gone away
was the cry, they asked no "favour," only fair play ;
they chose their line and kept it going as straight
as any man in the field.   The love of fox-hunting
must have been strong in all these ladies, especially
so, perhaps, in Mrs. Myddelton Biddulph, because
she had so far to travel by road before she reached
the Cheshire meets of Sir Watkin's hounds, which
she invariably attended whenever she was at Chirk
Castle.   Many a time have we seen her leave
Worthenbury at about 5 o'clock on a dark winter's

evening with a fourteen mile drive before her, over bad hilly roads, and the last mile a regular teazer ; nothing but a genuine love of sport could have caused her to go so far, and at so much personal inconvenience on the chance of a gallop.

In after years ladies became far more numerous in the hunting-field, and Sir Watkin's was usually represented by many of the fair sex who were worthy of distinction with any hounds in England ; among these we would name Miss Gill and her cousin Miss Scott, Mrs. and Miss Godsal, Mrs. Twyrwhitt Drake, Lady Cholmondeley, two Miss Warrens, Mrs. Hillyer Chapman, Mrs. Whitmore, Lady Alexander Paget, Mrs. Gordon Horton, Miss Heywood Lonsdale, though only a girl at that time, making a promise which she has certainly abundantly fulfilled, Miss M. Ethelston, the Misses Peel, and Lady Williams Wynn, of whom the poet wrote :—

> " Miss Wynn on her black
> Is with them, alack !
> The mare's tail is pointing this way.

Those grey hairs appear,
As I very much fear,
Our guides for the rest of the day."

Then, towards the close of Charles Payne's tenure of office, the two Misses Myddelton Biddulph appeared in Sir Watkin's hunting-field, and proved themselves worthy descendants of their grandmother, Mrs. Myddelton Biddulph, who distinguished herself so greatly in the early days of Sir Watkin Wynn; Miss Cowan, the Misses Percys, and indeed, many more, so that now there are as many ladies riding to hounds as there were ladies and gentlemen when Sir Watkin Wynn commenced hunting this country.

All these named, however, were bright examples of brilliant horsemanship. There are, we know, some others probably equally good, but they belong to the present day rather than that of which we write, so that we cannot speak of them from our personal knowledge.

WYNNSTAY.

CHAPTER VI.

"Oh, Sir Watkin's stout hounds
   Make the sweetest of sounds,
When a good fox is halloaed away;
   You may ride till you die,
   But you'll never come nigh
Those hounds, when they're once well away."

When Walker retired, Sir Watkin appointed
Charles Payne, of Pytchley celebrity, to succeed
him. "Baily," in 1860, writes of him in these
words: "I know of no man of the present time
enjoying in so high a degree the attributes of a
high-class huntsman as Charles Payne; he looks
what he is, and is what he looks, a superior sportsman, with a handsome, though determined countenance, betokening the inclination rather to command than obey, and yet there are few more civil
and obliging, except where his civility would be
thrown away. Payne has a very difficult card to
play with such a field as is usually seen with the

Pytchley Fox Hounds, and were it not for his firm-
ness of character, sport would be out of the question.
He is unmistakably there, the right man in the right
place; he has, moreover, done the country good
service by breeding for them as fine a pack of fox
hounds as any kennel can show."

We doubt not that everyone who hunted in this
country when Charles Payne took over the management of the Wynnstay Hounds will endorse the
opinion of the writer of this article, and admit that
Sir Watkin made a very happy choice.   Payne commenced his duties as huntsman at Wynnstay in 1865.

His style of riding to hounds and hunting them
was altogether different from that of Walker, yet
not less successful; indeed, when he realized the
difference in the country he had then to ride over
and hunt, from that of Northamptonshire, he showed
quite as much sport as John Walker had ever done,
and far more than he had done in his last two
seasons, when it needed no conjurer to tell, that
Walker ought to have been at home under a
doctor's care, instead of hunting a pack of fox

hounds; nothing but sheer pluck and a strong love of hunting a fox could have made him go on as long as he did.

We could find plenty of samples of the sport Payne showed directly he came to Wynnstay, but for the present content ourselves with an account sent us by Major Lloyd, of the Grenadier Guards (a keen lover of the great Goddess Diana, certainly hereditary), of an extraordinary run on Christmas Eve, 1865, from Aston Gorse, where they found at three o'clock in the afternoon and went away for the Mile House, Colonel Lloyd, Jack Jones and Payne with them; a large following in their wake. Away they went towards Whittington and Fernhill, crossed the railway past Trewern, and on to the hill near Sclattyn, but our gallant fox was not beaten yet, for he took, I won't say us, but the hounds, over the Llangollen Valley, and was pulled down in the quarries on the other side. Charles Payne got across the valley and met a man with the fox in his cart, who had seen the hounds kill him, drove them away and secured the prey.

Neither the time nor distance of this run is recorded, but it was talked of for years.

Charles Payne said it was the best run he ever saw.

Very soon after Payne began his first season of 1865-66, a great blight fell on this country, and especially on the grass or Cheshire side of it; we refer to the Rinderpest. This created a feeling of despondency over everyone connected with dairy farming, which is the prevailing industry of the district, and unfortunately a dread sprang up in the minds of some that this fearful scourge was spread by hounds and foxes. One large landed proprietor went so far as to destroy, it is reported, seventy foxes, though he was in ordinary times a good fox preserver.

Early in the new year Sir Watkin and Lady Williams Wynn went to Rome, and acting with his usual good sense, he left it to the tenant farmers to decide whether his hounds should go on hunting or the season close at once. The decision they arrived at was that hunting should continue as usual, as they thought that neither hounds nor foxes carried the infection, and we believe they were influenced in coming to this conclusion by the fact which we are told was brought before them, that whenever the hounds went *from* their kennels or *returned*, they passed through a herd of cows, which nevertheless escaped the pestilence. The farmers in Cheshire seem to have come to the same conclusion; Lord Grosvenor, who was then Master of the Cheshire Hounds (it was, we believe, his last season, when he was succeeded by Mr. Corbet), referred the matter to the Nantwich Board of Guardians, and they passed an unanimous resolution against the discontinuance of fox-hunting. Lord Grosvenor stated that throughout his hunt, he had only met one dissentient farmer.

It was indeed a sad and most depressing time, and the reality of it was often painfully brought home to us by seeing cattle lying dead in the field over which we were galloping after the hounds. Fortunately we all soon forget even the bitterest of our sorrows, and as it appeared to us, no national

Q

calamity was ever borne more heroically or sooner
forgotten than that of the Rinderpest; the farms
were soon restocked with cows from Wales, Holland,
or wherever the farmers could buy them, foxes
nearly as numerous as before, and smiling faces
welcomed Sir Watkin's hounds wherever they went.

It seems to have been the general opinion among
hound men that the Wynnstay kennels were at the
close of Walker's term of office too full of the
blood of Royal; indeed in 1867 we find in the
Wynnstay hound list seven couples by him, though
this was a trifle compared with Squire Osbaldeston,
having in his kennel *at one time* forty couples by his
Furrier. Payne, however, soon put this right, and
it was admitted on all sides that there was a great
improvement in the pack under the new management,
and he had besides in his first year's entry a great
addition in six noble looking hounds, bred of course
by Walker; perhaps six better looking brothers
never came at one birth from the same mother.
Their names were Rambler, Rawcliffe, Regent,
Rockwood, Romeo and Rufus; they were by Fitz-

CHARLES PAYNE.

william Regent out of Rally. Payne's favourite hound was Painter by the Duke of Rutland's Druid out of Posy; he was a badger-pied hound of great merit, very reliable, of medium size, and one that never tired.

Payne soon made a reputation for himself in this country, as he had in Northamptonshire, and secured not only the confidence of his master, but the approbation of all who hunted with him ; many good runs have we seen with him. Our diary records :—

10th January, 1867. " Out hunting at Bangor, a good run from Burton's Wood, but the hounds ran away from everyone. Hard frost the next day, which possibly accounted for the good scent."

2nd February. " At Carden, a first-rate day's sport from Royalty."

Major Lloyd tells of a good run from Babbin's Wood in this year, through Aston, past the lock ; the field got over the canal by the bridge close by, up to Knockin and on to Leighton Shelf. Charles Payne and the present Lord Hill (then Rowland Hill) had the best of it all the way, with my father galloping behind : I suppose halloaing. Also he recalls another run from Babbin's Wood, through Halston up to Colemere, where the fox was killed in the open.

18th February. " Ditto from Aldersey."

9th March. " Met at Worthenbury, had a good run from Burton's Wood and killed him in front of Knolton Hall, hounds crossed the Dee twice in this run, first by the Darland, next by the Eyton Ford. Did not find again till they drew the Cottage Gorse, crossed the River Dee a third time, and had a good run over the Isycoed country : fortunately the river was low."

In this year it was proposed to run the Bangor Hunt Steeplechases on the 12th March, but a heavy fall of snow stopped them.

A friend sends us an account of a good run with the Wynnstay Hounds on 7th January, 1868 : " Found our fox in Woodmill Coppice, ran to Oteley, Lea Woods, Wittal Moss, back past Wood Mill, through Penley, just skirting the dingles, leaving them on our left hand to Emral Park, which they crossed as if going to the Cottage Gorse, but he turned towards Worthenbury, leaving the village just on the right hand, went into the meadows, and the hounds caught him on the bank of the River Dee not far from Castletown Gorse; two hounds rolled with him into the river, but unfortunately the fox did not re-appear." Charles Payne's disappointment at the loss of his fox was only equalled by that of the hounds; over and over again he declared that he would rather have given five pounds *out of his own pocket*, than have lost him. This was the best run we ever saw in Sir Watkin's country, and the longest; the fox passed covert after covert from Wittal Moss without entering one, even the Penley Dingles had no charms for him. About eight men out of a large field saw the finish. Tom Smith's horse was so beaten that he could not get beyond the village of Worthenbury, neither would Charles Payne have been in at the death, had not that good sportsman, Colonel Rivers Bulkeley, whom Sir Watkin had mounted on a good little chestnut mare, which he bought from John Darby,

of Rugby, generously given her up and so enabled
Payne to see the end of his fox.

Perhaps the best season Sir Watkin's hounds ever
had during the many long years he so generously
hunted the country, was that of 1868-69 :—

On the 19th November we note " A capital run
from Broughton to Bettisfield."

28th November, " Met at Shocklach, a good day's
sport from Castletown and Barnston's Gorse.   Great
cheering for Sir Watkin on his arrival at the meet
on account of his election yesterday."

25th January, 1869.   " Out hunting at Farndon,
a capital day, killed in the open."

24th February.   " A very good gallop from
Carden and killed in the open."

2nd March.   " A real good day's sport from
Brynypys and killed in the open."

7th March.   " A capital day's sport from Broughton ; two foxes killed in the open.   The Duc de
Chartres and a large field out."

14th March.   " A very enjoyable gallop from the
Green Dragon, and killed in the open."

21st March. "Met at Malpas, killed a fox in the open after a good thirty-five minutes. Nothing else done."

This is a very good record from the diary of one who did not hunt very often, and, when he did, not always with Sir Watkin's hounds.

In the season of 1869-70, in the early part of it at all events, we do not find any record of "kills in the open," though there may have been many when we were not hunting; however, on 13th February, we have marked "a very hard day from Lightwood."

24th February. "A *good* run from Crewe Gorse to Bolesworth."

6th March. "Met at Bangor the day after the Steeplechases; a good run of an hour and a half from the Cottage Gorse over a bad country, then a very good but *ringing* run of an hour and a quarter from Chorlton." On the whole this season seems to have been only moderate to fair. *Baily's Magazine* says of it : " Sir Watkin Wynn's hounds have had a good average season's sport, still they have killed a good many more foxes than usual, as, since 2nd

November, sixteen brace have been killed, and eight and a half brace run to ground, which is by no means a bad return list, particularly as he had been very unlucky with his kennel servants, Harry Tocock having dislocated his ankle during cub hunting, and not having been on a horse since."

In 1870-71, matters improved. We find in our diary these entries :—

4th November. "A capital day's sport from Carden over a very good country."

2nd December. "A good run from Campbell's Gorse to ground close to Ellesmere Station."

15th January. "A first rate run of one hour and thirty minutes, then a second run of an hour. *Very good.*"

17th January. "A very good run from Aldersey, killed our fox in the open near Grafton Gorse."

Then hunting was stopped by frost and snow till

21st February. "Met at Holt, a very good hunting run from Royalty, and a fast gallop from Castletown."

4th March. "Met at Carden. A good day's

sport from there and Grafton Gorse; killed near Hanmer."

The spring of this year was unusually dry, and the ground very hard, nevertheless the hounds had a "good fair day's sport from Iscoed Park, 29th March, considering the dry state of the ground."

3rd April. Notwithstanding that there had been no rain, good runs are recorded from the Wyches, Burton's Wood, and Campbell's Gorse, with the comment "a very hard day for horses." This probably finished the season.

Many more good runs might be added, but we fear to weary those who may wade through these pages. We add, however, the following from a letter, of Mr. Arthur Whieldon, ex M.F.H., who kindly sent a subscription towards a charitable object connected with fox-hunting. In mentioning the river Dee his words are, "I must soon expect to cross a more unfathomable river (the Styx)," and adds, "this recalls to mind that memorable day when we found at Sutton Green Covert a good fox which crossed at once the river Dee. I was then a

R

complete stranger to the country, and finding myself
at the end of one of those large meadows, with the
river Dee in flood staring me in the face, did not
know which way to turn, when Charles Payne
beckoned me to follow him, which I did to the ferry
boat. This, however, could scarcely contain Payne,
myself, the two whippers-in and our horses, being
full to the gunwale, and rocking to and fro fearfully ;
and the recent fate of Sir Charles Sligsby (1869)
came vividly before my mind's eye, for we were all
but foundering, the old woman at the wheel, dead
beaten, having left us to our fate in the middle ot
the stream, shouting out she could do no more.
Then that good fellow, Tom Smith, pluckily jumped
into the middle of the flood, scrambled ashore, and
pulled us safely over. We skeltered along for miles,
a long stern chase in pursuit of the hounds, and
when we reached them, you and myself represented
the numerous field of the morning ; nor have I
forgotten how you good-naturedly took compassion
on my poor exhausted steed and lent me one of your
own to carry me home, hæc olim meminisse Juvabit."

Well do we remember the day mentioned, we had not intended to hunt, and were sitting at our table writing, when our old butler, John Webb, rushed in, saying " The hounds are coming over the meadows in full cry, and not a soul with them." To mount a horse and gallop after them seemed but the work of a few minutes, and soon we got up to the hounds, but no one joined the chase till we reached the Castle Hill in the Wyches, and then Charles Payne and our friend appeared. Anyone who has ever seen the river Dee in flood, will readily acknowledge that this feat of Tom Smith's, in jumping into it to the rescue of his comrades, was as plucky a deed as ever was done in or out of the hunting-field, and if there was such a thing as a Victoria Cross for deeds of daring, *not* on the battle-field, assuredly Tom Smith ought to have had it.

There is no date given to the event which our friend records, but we have reason to believe it was towards the end of the season of 1870-71, the first season Tom Smith came to Wynnstay. No better whipper-in than Tom ever hallaoed a fox away from

a covert, or turned a hound to a huntsman. He
left Sir Watkin's country in 1877 to the great
regret of every man hunting in it; since which
time he has been hunting the Bramham Moor
Hounds for that distinguished sportsman Mr. George
Lane-Fox, where he is as popular with everyone as
he was here.

Charles Payne was especially fortunate in retain-
ing one as long as he did, so well deserving of
promotion.

In the season of 1871-72, the elements were
decidedly unfavourable to the sport of fox-hunting;
there were several weeks of frost and snow, then a
very boisterous March and a remarkably dry April.
They began very well, however, " with a *good* day's
sport from Aldersey to Eaton " on the 15th November, then a fast gallop from Castletown in the afternoon.

26th December they had again " a good day's
sport from Aldersey," " another run from Royalty,
and a third from Castletown."

It is only fair to add as a comment on our diary

that we seldom mark in it the death of a fox unless
he is fairly caught in the open ; an ordinary kill in
a covert is almost invariably omitted.

Major Lloyd sends us an account of a run at this
time from the Fenns, whence the fox took them past
Bettisfield and Gredington, over the Old Hall property, and leaving Burton's Wood on the right to
ground in the Wyches ; he adds, the hounds went at
great pace all the way, and had far the best of us ;
it was a real case of galloping. Two incidents connected with this run, fix it, he says, indelibly in my
mind. The first was an extremely unpleasant one ;
I was riding a good young thoroughbred, but somewhat sticky. My father was on a high-class hunter.
When nearing the Wyches, we came to a small
brook, with boggy banks, and knowing my horse
wanted a lead, I followed my father, and "woe
worth the hour, and woe worth the day," he fell, and
I jumped on him ! I draw a veil over what followed.
My horse was so lame that with difficulty I got him
home ; my father's scarcely lame at all ; in a week
mine was quite sound, but his took to running joint

oil and died. The second incident was our meeting old Walker, to whom my father said, " A first-rate run ;" " I know it," said he, " I was on the road and heard them running 'great guns' over the Old Hall." I never saw him again, and the next I heard of him was his death and burial on the day the hounds had the run of the season. He adds another run with a characteristic anecdote of our M.F.H. When the hounds were running in the Carden country, they crossed the Aldersey brook ; up to this point my father had been quite in front on a good horse called Telegram ; he would not, however, face water, and my father knew it, so he pulled up, and looking round, spied his second horseman, to whom he shouted, "Come on, ride him at it." The man did as he was told, and cleared it easily. "Get off," said my father ; he himself jumped off Telegram, crawled on a pole over the brook, and was soon alone with the hounds. " How did Dick get there ?" said Sir Watkin, and when he was told, · out came the handkerchief, and into his mouth it went. My father never heard the last of it.

In the season of 1872-73, we find we were frequently absent from home, so no doubt missed a good deal of sport, but we were present on the 7th December, when they "had a good day from Cloverley and Styche."

26th December. "Met at Aldersey, killed him near Chester. Another run from Royalty. A good day."

11th January. "Met at Malpas, found a good fox at Edge, and killed him close to Aldersey Hall in the open ; found again in Castletown, and had quite a first-rate gallop to the Cheshire Hills. Home late. About the best day of the season."

28th February. "A good ringing run from Castletown of one hour and thirty minutes."

24th March. "A first-rate gallop from Grafton." This run ended in a kill near the Beachin, after about fifty-five minutes.

This appears to have been a very long and successful season, which ended on April 17th with "a good run from the Cottage Gorse to Penley," Bangor Hunt Steeplechases coming off the next day (18th April).

Season 1874-75.

6th November. "A good run from Borras Wood."

17th November. "A fine run from Randles Gorse to Crewe Gorse."

1st January. "Late in the day a good run from Sir Roger Palmer's Gorse. Home late."

14th January. "A very good day from Broughton."

21st April. "Hunted from Chirk Castle, but not much sport."

Season 1875-76.

6th November. "A good run from Carden Cliff to Hanmer, past Broughton and Burton's Wood."

They had a good run from Cox's Wood past Borras to the Gerwyn, and thence to ground in Park Eyton.

24th November. "A good gallop from Iscoed to Broughton Gorse."

25th November. We find this entry in our diary.—"Rode over to Wynnstay to say good-bye to Sir Watkin, who was going abroad for the winter."

30th January. "A long ringing run from Royalty all over that country for two hours and a half."

2nd February. "A very good day's sport from Acton."

9th February. "A good hunting run from Grafton; left off at Eaton."

14th February. "A good day's sport from Erddig."

27th March. "A real good gallop with an out-lying fox from near Larges."

We have marked this in our diary as a moderate season, and it says : "Sir Watkin away, and we seem not only to have lost a genial friend, but he appears to have taken the scent of the fox with him."

1876-77.

26th January. "A real good run from the Wyches, and killed in the open. Then found in Burton's Wood, and had a good ring past Broughton and Larges to the Wyches."

Ran from Belmont through Fernhill, Halston,

8

Woodhouse, nearly to Boreatton, but turning to the right, lost our fox near Stanwardine, after a very fast run with a twelve-mile point.

6th March. "Met at Bangor, found in the Cottage Gorse, ran to Cuddington, thence to Burton's Wood; a clinker and a kill."

24th March. "A good day from Larges and the Wyches."

7th April. "Met at Worthenbury; found an out-lying fox in a meadow below the Rectory; a pretty gallop towards Cherry Hill; then found in the Cottage Gorse and ran to Lightwood."

19th April. "Sir Watkin out; met at Eaton, a nice run from Royalty."

21st April. Bangor Steeplechases.

22nd April. "Hunted at Brynypys; heard the cuckoo; a strong hint to leave off hunting."

During the early part of 1877, Sir Watkin's health caused the gravest anxiety to his friends, and we miss him from the hunting-field all January and February, but we find that he was out hunting on 22nd March, when his hounds met at Wynnstay,

and again on 31st March. Soon after this time he
went for a tour through Spain, when we received
the following characteristic letter from him, dated
24th April; the post mark supplies the year—1877.

" Lisbon.

" DEAR P.,—

" Been to Church ; going to the races ; done
two days' bull-fighting; drank any amount of sherry.
Had a good sea voyage, though it was a little rough
I was very regular at my meals. I will try to be at
Chester to tell you the news. I go to-morrow to
Grenada, then Madrid, Bordeaux, Paris; can I do
anything for you anywhere?

" Yours sincerely,
" W. W. W."

Unfortunately Sir Watkin never dated his letters,
therefore the difficulty is where to place them ; however, we venture to give this other one, which was
evidently written when he went in his steam yacht
to the East.

"Constantinople,

Dear P.,—   "April 3.

"Thanks for your's. All my letters were sent, by mistake, from Smyrna to Alexandria, back here through three-quarters of the globe, so if you hear me abused for not answering letters you can give my excuse. Glad you have had good sport; wish I had been with you instead of riding miserable brutes here; still, have had no casualties, but with wretched tackle and most moderate animals it was more luck than cunning. So Miss —— is to be married; our hunting young ladies get passed on. M. is delighted with yachting, and only complains when she goes on shore. A. is very unwell when there is anything of a sea; she was, however, much interested with her journey to Jerusalem and Damascus; I have my own ideas of certain things in the Bible from what I have seen. I have got what would make a good ' Penny Reading ' in my head. Hope to see you at Bangor.

"Yours sincerely,

" W. W. W."

There was an amusing story told of Sir Watkin's arrival at Gibraltar after leaving England on this trip. When his yacht cast anchor he put on some hunting clothes, and by arrangement, as soon as he got on shore mounted a horse which was sent to meet him, and had a day with the Garrison Hounds there, which we believe were then hunted by a son of Charles Payne's.

Bangor Steeplechases were held in fine weather on the 12th April, 1878, with swallows flying about.

In November and December of the season of 1878-79, Sir Watkin had a little hunting, but on the 30th December he came over here to make some hunting arrangements, as he was going abroad for the winter. We returned with him to Wynnstay for luncheon, and all that occurred that day is impressed upon our mind by the fact that during the time spent on the road between Bangor and Wynnstay and the return there, a heavy flood had come over the Bangor Road, of which we knew nothing until we found Sir Watkin's brougham half full of water.

The new year (1879) began *very well* with a good

gallop from Gredington to Oteley, on which day they killed a fox close to Llannerch Panna. Frost the next day, and hunting stopped till 10th February.

12th February. " A nice day from Clutton's and Large's Gorse."

19th February. " A good day's sport from Tom Iron's and Mr. Leche's Gorse."

18th March. " Another from Macefen and caught him."

19th March. " A pretty gallop from Royalty to Eaton."

25th April. Bangor Steeplechases.

1879-80.

In November there were very severe frosts ; seventeen degrees on the 3rd December. This frost lasted from the 14th November until the 27th December, and it returned unabashed in January till well into February. · There is more notice in our diary this year of skating than fox-hunting.

On 23rd December, 1880, we had a good run from Burton's Wood, when the hounds killed their fox at Shocklach. The hounds met that day at Iscoed.

25th February, 1881. Hounds met at Carden, the Empress out.

30th March, 1881. Hounds met at Worthenbury; a good day; Sir Watkin and several others came in at the end of the day.

During this season we have noted that Sir Watkin was able to ride with his hounds very little; he generally went with them in his carriage. In the season of 1880-81, the Empress of Austria rented Combermere Abbey from Lord Combermere, as she also did in the following year, 1881-82. She hunted occasionally then with Sir Watkin's hounds, though more generally with the Cheshire, and we believe sometimes with the North Staffordshire. When she first came into this neighbourhood " Bay " Middleton was her pilot; afterwards Colonel Rivers Bulkeley showed her the way, and from his knowledge of the country and fine · horsemanship, well deserved the compliment she was wont to pay him : " Thank you, Colonel Bulkeley, I have been with the hounds to-day."

Her Imperial Majesty's charming appearance and gracious manners made her right welcome in the hunting-field, and her magnificent expenditure was greatly missed in the neighbourhood of Whitchurch when she gave up Combermere Abbey.

We never heard who selected the horses Her Majesty rode, but they struck us as a very well bred, useful looking lot, and they seemed to do their work remarkably well.

During her stay at the Abbey she paid a visit to Wynnstay and the Kennels, and also to Eaton and the Duke of Westminster's paddocks to see his thoroughbred stock, and at each of these places she left behind her *brilliant* marks of her appreciation of the attention paid her by Charles Payne, Simpson, and Mr. Chapman, the Duke's stud manager.

We did not hunt much at this time for domestic reasons, but went to meets at Carden, Broughton, and Iscoed to see the Empress's "turn out"; her horses and her habits were the envy of all the ladies who hunted with these hounds, and her habits, we are told, they did try and copy, but we neither *saw* nor heard of anyone imitating her custom of carrying her fan into the hunting-field, which, however, she did with a grace peculiar to herself.

Her own pad groom put her on her saddle, having first taken off his hat and placed it on some convenient, but distant spot. Sir Watkin was on horseback occasionally with her, and certainly when the hounds met at Carden, and showed her all the attention due to her Imperial rank and beauty ; but his hunting career was almost ended, though the bright episode of Her Majesty's brief sojourn in the country seemed to cause him to rouse himself to receive her in a fitting way, perhaps even more than his strength would admit.

The last time we ever saw Sir Watkin in the hunting-field on horseback was on the 7th April, 1883, when the hounds met at Gresford, and as there was no sport, we had frequent opportunities of seeing what ravages disease had made in him ; his clothes hung about him, and to a large extent his spirits, hitherto good, had left him. For the last four or five years he had but seldom seen his own hounds

T

in the hunting-field, and consequently had little or no return in personal amusement for his magnificent expenditure on his hunting establishment.

At the close of the season, 1882-83, Charles Payne finished his successful career with the Wynnstay Hounds, and singular to say, he also, as John Walker had done before him, carried the horn for eighteen seasons in Sir Watkin Wynn's service.

We have mentioned how fortunate John Walker was with Sir Watkin's horses. Although we have not enquired of the old servants at Wynnstay whether they can give the name or names of any other horse or horses which Charles Payne killed out hunting, *we* can only remember one unfortunate accident of this kind, and that was with a mare called Rebecca, which we believe Sir Watkin bought from Mr. Wilbraham Tollemache, of Dorfold. She was an undeniable " fencer," and we often take friends to see an extraordinary jump she made over a most dangerous fence on the morning she was killed, yet she broke her back over a *very small gap* into a green lane near Mr. Brassey's of Cuddington.

With his accustomed generous consideration, Sir
Watkin gave Payne a pension, which we heartily
wish he may live to enjoy for many years to
come. His services, too, were generally appreciated
throughout the country over which he hunted, the
outcome of which was the gratifying testimonial of
£1,379, which was presented to him by Lord
Combermere and Mr. Heywood Lonsdale, in the
presence of a numerous gathering of covert owners,
friends, and tenant farmers, all anxious to bear their
testimony to the attention and civility of Charles
Payne, and the sport he had shown in the hunting-
field for so many years.

In addition to the sum named, he had given him
a silver hunting horn, and an address on vellum in
an oak frame :—

"Presented to Charles Payne on Thursday, 26th
July, 1883. the sum of thirteen hundred and seventy-
nine pounds four shillings, including the cost of a
silver hunting horn and this address, by members
of the Wynnstay Hunt and other friends, as an
expression of their high appreciation of his uniform

civility and constant endeavour to show sport
during the eighteen years he hunted Sir Watkin
Wynn's hounds."

CHAPTER VII.

' The honours of a name 'tis just to guard,
    They are a trust but lent us, which we take,
    And in reverence to the donor's fame,
    With care transmit to other hands."

SHIRLEY.

On Charles Payne's retirement, Sir Watkin
appointed Frank Goodall, who had been hunting
the Meath, a member of, perhaps, the most
celebrated "huntsman" family in England, to fill
his post. Unfortunately for Goodall, he missed the
kindly support and watchful eye of his master, who
was then unable to go out with his own hounds
except on wheels, and was frequently prevented by
illness from even doing this. Many of those who
had hunted for years with the Wynnstay pack were
anxious, in the absence of the master, to have a
voice in the arrangement of the day's sport, and as
Goodall could not possibly carry out the wishes of
them all, he consequently made some of them any-

thing but friendly to him; added to this, his manners were scarcely so good as those of some of his family; however, as far as we were able to judge, we never saw any huntsman more anxious to show sport than he was, or enjoy a run more than he did. A bold horseman, quick in getting away with his fox, with most of the attributes of a good huntsman, from the causes named he was scarcely a success, and yet he showed a great deal of sport during the two seasons he was at Wynnstay.

Lord Waterford was hunting with the Wynnstay Hounds during the season of 1883-84. His magnificent stud of weight-carrying hunters was, we fear, the cause of making even Christian fox-hunters break the tenth commandment. We lost a good sportsman and a fine horseman when he migrated to Leicester-shire.

There were many good runs during this season, which was a very open one, hounds being only prevented hunting three or four days the second week in December. Lord Waterford said it was the best season's hunting he ever remembered, all the neighbouring packs having equally good sport.

The Honble. George Gore sends the following runs :—

Nov. 17th. Hounds met at Whitchurch in a pouring rain, trotted to Sandford, found in the csiers and ran straight up to Ightfield, bearing to the right past Cloverley Gorse up to Shavington Wall, where our fox turned back and made for Ash Covert ; did not go into it, but took us on to Osmere, and ended our run in Peel's Gorse ; a very good hunting run of one hour and three quarters.

Dec. 5th. Hounds at Broughton had a very fast gallop from Castletown, through Larges, nearly up to Malpas, but bearing to the right, went into the Wyches, where we got on fresh foxes. The first 25 minutes very fast.

Dec. 27th, Carden. Hounds slipped away from the Cliff without anyone with them, and hunted their fox at a great pace to ground in a rabbit hole just below Malpas. Found our next fox in Mrs. Leche's Gorse, which we hunted to Crewe, then on through Royalty, nearly up to Aldersey, but bearing to the right, he took us a ring round Barton, eventually beating us after a very nice 45 minutes.

Dec. 29th, Whitchurch. We had a very fast 30 minutes from Styche over the Losford Brook, which caused a good deal of grief, our fox eventually beating us amongst the intricate rocks in Hawkstone.

Jan. 12th, 1884, Ightfield. Found in Sandford, and ran our fox through Losford to Stoke Heath, in the Shropshire country, on through Colehurst Wood, and eventually killed him in the open at Woodseaves, after a clinking hour and 20 minutes. Found our next fox in Styche—I fancy the same we ran from there a fortnight ago, as he took us exactly the same line over the Losford Brook, marking him to ground in Hawkstone Park. This day, taking it all round, was the best day's sport of the season.

At this time (1884) *Baily* writes thus of Sir Watkin :—

" This Prince of Sportsmen has devoted his life to the Wynnstay country, and the result needs no telling ; his Whitchurch Saturdays draw crowds of the best men that Shropshire, Cheshire, and the

Welsh border countries can produce, and every farmer, as well as every landowner, combines to preserve foxes for Sir Watkin. Look at them now as they draw Ash Gorse—more than two hundred horsemen huddled together and the halloa, 'gone away,' sounds down wind, every knee clips its saddle and away they go—the Cloverley Brook hinders them scarce a moment, and those large rush grown pastures are flown over like lightning, and the hairy fences flicked through without hesitation. If the truth were known we believe Mr. Reginald Corbet enjoys his bye-day, minus the cares of office, quite as much as his screaming twenty minutes from Baddiley Gorse. Frank Goodall is getting more and more at home with his field, and though he lacks the winning ways of Charles Payne, he is a huntsman by nature; he misses much his master's aiding eye."

Alas, that master was to hunt no more. The precarious state of his health was known to every member of his hunt, and at every meet of his hounds the question was anxiously asked, "What news of Sir Watkin, is he better?"

U

In the *Baily* from which we have already quoted, we find an account of another Whitchurch Saturday. " Then again there was the day from Sandford, when scarcely a corner of Shropshire or Cheshire was unrepresented; *the* run was from Styche, when the fox made for Tern Hill, but bent to the right hand until Losford Brook came in the line—enough to try the nerve of the stoutest. After a fine run of an hour and twenty minutes, he got to ground on Nicco Hill."

At the close of the season of 1883-84, Sir Watkin went up to London, as usual, to his residence in St. James's Square, where he was among the victims of the dynamite outrage on the 30th May, which caused such a shock to London on that day. While sitting in his drawing room about ten o'clock in the evening, a fearful explosion was both felt and heard, which shattered most of the stone work in front of his house, and caused the greatest alarm to all the inmates of it. Most fortunately no member of the household or family was injured. Sir Watkin's nerve was always very good, and *apparently* he stood the shock very well, and was none the worse for it, yet it was the general opinion among his friends that in his *then* enfeebled state of health this frightful incident had a most injurious effect upon him. On the same evening, and nearly at the same hour, there was a similar attack made upon the Junior Carlton Club, which on one side faces St. James's Square, and it was on this side the dynamite was placed. The sound from this explosion also must have been plainly heard by all who were in Sir Watkin's house at the time. Unfortunately, fourteen servants were injured, some of them most seriously; one poor girl losing both her legs by this miscreant's diabolical work. It was thought that the wretch who placed the bomb against Sir Watkin's house made a mistake in the number, and intended to destroy the adjoining one, which was then in the occupation of the Government; a similar mistake having also been made in the case of the Junior Carlton Club, as the bomb placed against it was manifestly intended for Adair House, which then belonged to the War Department, but is now pulled down and added to the Club.

In consequence of the partial destruction of his house in St. James's Square, Sir Watkin at once left London for Wynnstay, and when we called on him on our return from Ashtead we were told Sir Watkin was at home, but it was then found that he had been taken from the house by the stable entrance and gone to Paddington Station. There were a great many servants in the hall when we entered, all with their travelling cloaks on, and one of the girls, when asked if they had felt the explosion very much, and what she thought it was, answered, "Fearfully! I thought it was the last day."

When the damage done to his house had been made good in some measure, Sir Watkin and Lady Williams Wynn returned to town, but with the ravages of disease on him more apparent to the eyes of his friends than ever.

In the season of 1884-85, *Baily's Magazine* reports Sir Watkin's stables as in wonderful form at this time, "not a lame horse among the lot, though they began cub-hunting in August. The opening day of regular hunting in the vale was at

Carden, which must be marked with a white stone.

November 8th, 1884. When they ran a fox from the Cliff to ground in Handley Gorse. Found again in Royalty, a covert which had not been drawn for two seasons, a good dog fox, who went away straight into the north Cheshire country for Saighton ; leaving it on the left, he made for Crow's Nest, but the hounds ran into him before he reached that covert, thirty-five minutes over the cream of the Cheshire Vale, with the Aldersey Brook thrown in.

On the 29th November, met at Iscoed Park ; the morning's work showed that Mr. Godsal's care of his coverts was not thrown away, for there were soon plenty of foxes on foot, and when Goodall threw his hounds into the covert near Kiln Green, though one went to ground, another, and a good one too, faced all the horsemen, and made straight for the Wyches, then turned towards Tushingham and Macefen, skirted Bar Mere, crossed the Tarporley Road, and over Norbury Common to ground in Wrenbury Moss, one of Mr. Corbet's coverts, after a good gallop of fifty minutes.

November 12th. Met at Broughton. We had another nice day over the vale, the best thing of the day being from Sourbutts over much the same country we went the previous Saturday. To-day, however, we failed to account for our fox, most of the field, including the huntsman, being pounded at the Aldersey Brook; hounds being left to themselves, were unable to hit off the line, after crossing the Eaton drives near Saighton.

December 6th. An excellent day was enjoyed. The best run was the last, an out and home gallop, one hour and seven minutes long, and ten miles in extent. The famous Ash Wood provided the material for the day's amusement. First one went as straight as a dart to Shavington, three and a half miles in a quarter of an hour, right through the extensive demesne and out on the Market Drayton side, where the fox, instead of turning back, ran outside, skirted the water, and faced the open in the south Cheshire country ; leaving Kent's rough on the right, he ran by Wilkesley, and then back to Ash, where the hounds were whipped off close to the

Wood, as it was nearly dark. Altogether we found four foxes that day in Ash Wood, three of which were killed.

During this season Sir Watkin went out occasionally in his brougham to see his hounds and have a talk with his neighbours, and he came to lunch with us on the 10th January, 1885, and again on 14th February, but the end was evidently near. On the 4th April we went to see him at Wynnstay, when he remarked that he was " a poor creature." Our diary's comment on this visit is, " Sir W. W. very ill."

A friend at this time writes thus of him : " I saw Sir Watkin in London three times ; his appearance shocked me, death is written in his face, I never expect to see him again."

About this time, what *Baily* described as "an interesting ceremony" was enacted at Wynnstay : " Sir Watkin's portrait, by Herkomer, R.A., was presented to his daughter, Mrs. Herbert Williams Wynn, by four hundred hunting men in the neighbourhood, as a wedding present. Such a gathering in the fine old Park with the hounds in the foreground, has not been witnessed since many years ago, when Sir Watkin had his picture presented to him, accompanied by Lady Wynn and a favourite hound, after the destruction by fire of the old Wynnstay Mansion. To-day, the Honble. Edward Kenyon made the presentation in most appropriate terms, and it cost Sir Watkin many an effort to overcome an overwhelming feeling of gratitude in replying to this token of his friends' good feeling towards himself and his family. It grieved us to see him such a confirmed invalid, for where throughout the length and breadth of England and Wales can you find his like, one who for forty years has kept a princely establishment and hunted a four day a week country extending through four counties, entirely at his own expense, while at the same time he has represented his native county, Denbighshire, in the House of Commons for a still longer period."

It seems a work of supererogation to try and add anything to the above, which indeed was the universal judgment of the neighbourhood; and the affection, respect and regard felt by *all* for Sir

Watkin, seemed to increase as they slowly realised how near his end was.

Bailey's Van, June, 1885, published then, but evidently written the previous month, writing of this picture, says : " At the Royal Academy there stood just before me the old familiar face of Sir Watkin Wynn, so truthful and lifelike, I could not refrain from blessing the art of Herkomer in having painted it. Howbeit, I turned away from the picture with a sigh, as I remembered how altered he had looked on the day we had given to his daughter and her husband this identical picture. As I jumped on my horse after the presentation, it was with a certain consciousness that I should never see that worthy man again in this life.

" No sooner had I left the Academy than an evening paper announced that Sir Watkin Wynn had gone from us.

" What a type of unassuming nobility he had been. What hearty good nature and sterling common sense had ever been harboured in that broad chest and cheery countenance. What a void

v

has his death created wherever Dee and Severn roll their swiftest waters. What a glorious example was he of Tennyson's words :

> " And thus he bore without abuse,
> The grand old name of Gentleman."

" A master of hounds without a subscription almost from his coming of age, a Member of Parliament for hardly a less period, the owner of many square miles not easily reckoned, a Deputy Lieutenant of four counties, a Provincial Grand Master of Freemasons, an Aide-de-Camp to the Queen, a Member of the Jockey Club, and a Great Western Director, a veritable Prince among Welshmen, and beloved by all.

" Just a few words of Sir Watkin Wynn as a master of foxhounds. Though never a flyer he had an extraordinary knack of getting over the country. He would creep through blind places, drop his horse into a road, jump the Aldersey Brook at a stand; never lose the line of his hounds. In his hey-day he always rode big horses, but latterly he had ridden strong cobby horses and

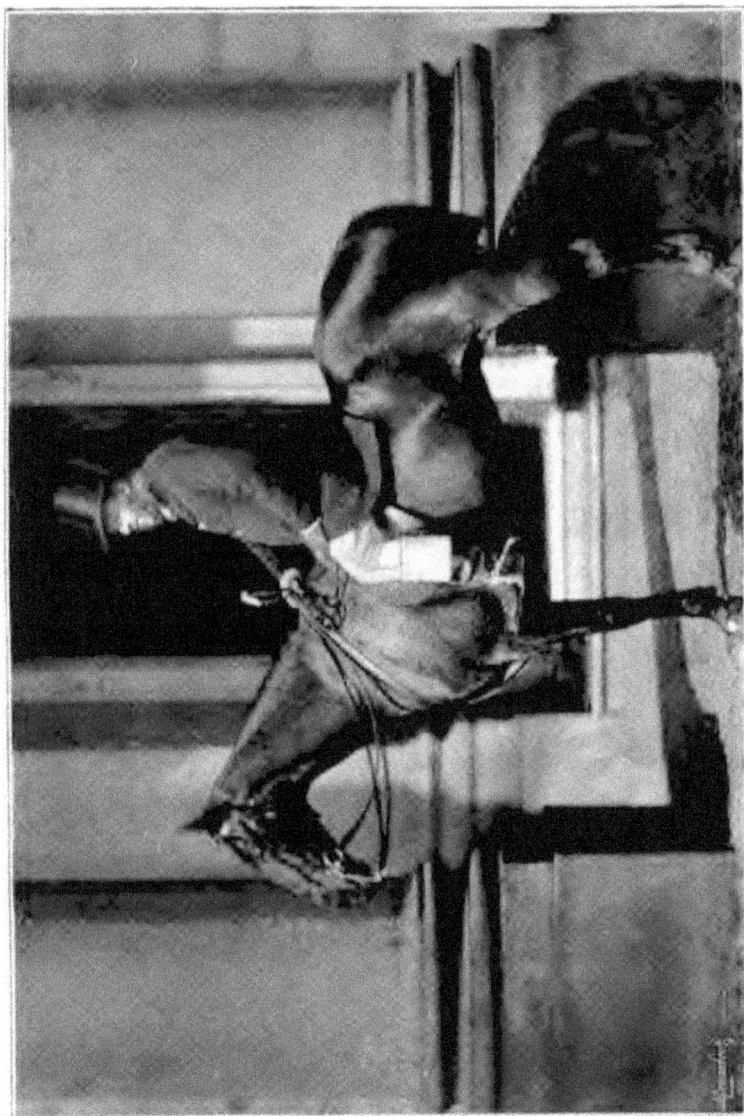

SIR WATKIN WYNN.

tested their understandings pretty well down all sorts of roads, that younger and lighter men would have shuddered at, with a loose rein at full gallop. Innumerable stories are told of Sir Watkin, illustrating his good nature and sportsmanlike qualities."

The writer of this excellent article, however, has not favoured us with any one of these stories, so we venture to add one, which we know is true, and which caused great amusement at the time it took place, which was only a few years before Sir Watkin's death. When travelling on a certain occasion by the Cambrian Railway, a gentleman fell into conversation with Sir Watkin, and finding that he knew thoroughly all the country through which they passed repeatedly asked, " Whose property is this?" and on each occasion received the same answer —" Mine." When they reached the terminus where the gentleman was leaving the railway, he thought it would only be fair to the Company to give the guard a friendly hint, so he advised him to keep an eye on his fellow-traveller, saying, " He is *evidently a lunatic*, as he had claimed as his own all the farms by the side of the railway line for *miles*."

We saw Sir Watkin for the last time on 1st May; he was then very ill, and knew perfectly well his end was near, and on the morning of the 9th May, when at breakfast, a telegram from Wynnstay was sent to us : "Sir Watkin passed away quietly at a quarter to two this morning." On the 15th May we saw him peacefully laid in his grave in the pretty little churchyard at Llangedwyn, near his dear little daughter Nesta, whose life had been so short, and who yet had made herself so beloved.

Every friend Sir Watkin had in the world seemed to be at Llangedwyn on this occasion, and a scene more sad we have seldom witnessed. We realised our loss, and the thought of it cast a chill upon us all.

The same friend who wrote as to Sir Watkin's state of health then wrote : "The end has come sooner than I expected. Poor old chap, we shall never see his like again; he was more than an individual, he was an institution ; his loss in your neighbourhood is simply irreparable."

This, without doubt, was the opinion of us all.

"Quis desiderio sit pudor aut modus, tam cari capitis." Nothing that we can write can better describe than the word "irreparable," the loss of our M.F.H., Sir Watkin Williams Wynn; he left a name which is venerated by all who had the honour of his acquaintance or the privilege of his friendship. As a master of fox hounds he could not be excelled, and it is in that capacity that we have ventured to write of him; but it would be less than justice, if we did not add that he was a loyal friend, a kind and genial acquaintance, a generous and indulgent land-lord, and a most considerate master.

Shortly before his death Sir Watkin appointed Lockey as his huntsman, though unhappily he did not live to see him in the hunting-field; but the best proof we can give that the choice was a happy one is that he continues in the service of the present Sir Watkin Wynn, who hunts the country in the same munificent—and, we believe successful—way as his uncle; but the doings of his pack we must leave to some other to describe, most heartily wishing him every success as Master of the Wynnstay Hounds.

CHAPTER THE LAST.

"A toast to every heart is speaking
Health to all friends round the Wrekin."

Shropshire to wit.

Fox-hunting appears to have taken root both in North and South Shropshire in very early days, probably about the middle of the last century ; Mr. Forester of Willey taking the lead in the south, while Mr. Hill of Prees and Mr. Corbet of Sundorne Castle held the north.   Mr. Randall, in his interesting book ("Old Sports and Sportsmen") tells us that the Willey pack, hunted from the Clee Hills to the Needles eye on the Wrekin ; he does not, however, fix a date when these hounds were established at Willey, but probably we shall not be very wide of the mark if we name 1770 as the time.

Hunting in those days was a very different thing from what it now is ; assuredly it was no sluggard's work, for at the hour of 4 a.m those who were going out would be found preparing their inner man for the chase by a breakfast of underdone beef, with eggs beaten up in brandy to fill up the interstices ; then in the Willey days away went Mr. Forester with a host of friends of the same stamp, followed by his celebrated whipper-in Tom Moody, all ready to follow wherever bold Reynard led the way. Some extraordinary runs are recorded of these hounds, one especially with a fox they called " Old Tinker," whose brush the Squire was especially anxious to handle ; but though fair and unfair means were resorted to, Old Tinker beat them, only, however, to die ignominiously in a drain, where he was found the following week, poor wretch, after being hunted until the huntsman's horse was too blown to follow ; ten couples of fresh hounds were let loose on his track, Moody's horse fell dead under him, and the hounds were too tired to pursue him further.

Those were jovial days, and a meet at Willey drew together a large field to partake of the Squire's hospitality ; as many as the hall would accommodate arrived the afternoon before, mounted on their hunters, and wearing the boots and breeches they were to appear in the following morning. A night of rollicking fun, extending to the small hours, appears to have been the invariable sequel, then after an hour or two of bed, or possibly on a sofa, away they went at early dawn to get on the trail of a fox.

Tom Moody, who evidently was a ruling spirit in the hunting-field, entered Squire Forester's service as a youth. The Squire saw him trying to ride a colt over a gate, and persevere until he got him over; this showed the stuff Tom was made of, so he was taken into the Willey stables, and at length was made whipper-in, but he never rose higher, though his fine nerve, and keen love of fox-hunting caused him to be considered by his master, and those who knew him in the hunting-field, as the best whipper-in in England.

Tom's name is immortalised by Dibdin, who probably had hunted with him when he was a guest at Willey. When the Squire thereof gave up his hounds, Tom migrated to Sundorne Castle, but either the climate of North Shropshire or the *ale*, did not suit his constitution, so he once more returned to Willey.

We are all familiar with the picture representing poor Tom Moody's obsequies, which were conducted rather under fox-hunting rules than on any burial ritual with which we are acquainted. The account given us is this :

" In December, 1796, was buried at Barrow, near Wenlock, Thomas Moodie, the well-known whipper-in to G. Forester's foxhounds for twenty years. He was carried to his grave by six "earthstoppers"; and directly after the corpse followed his favourite horse, carrying his last fox's brush in the front of his bridle, with his cap, whip, boots, spurs and girdle across the saddle. The ceremony over, by his express desire, three view halloas were given over his grave ; and so ended poor Tom, an honest, faithful fellow, and a real genuine sportsman of a class that has now quite died out."

When Squire Forester gave up hunting, the farmers of the district appear to have kept the

w

hounds on, probably as a "trencher-fed" pack,
collected from their various homes by the sound of
a horn the night before hunting, plentifully supplied
with water, and dismissed by a cut of a whip to
their several quarters at the end of the day's sport.

In North Shropshire, for some years before the
close of the last century, Mr. Hill, of Prees, had a
pack of hounds, as well as Mr. Corbet, of Sundorne.
The latter, however, was by far the best known of
the two, in fact, very little is known of Mr. Hill or
his hounds, though we find some of them in Mr.
Corbet's hound lists. Before the close of the last
century, Mr. Corbet hunted all the country north of
the Severn, but like his friend and neighbour, Sir
Richard Puleston, he found there were not foxes
enough in his country to engage the attention of his
hounds for a whole season, so when Mr. Warde
gave up hunting the Warwickshire country in 1792,
Mr. Corbet took his hounds to Stratford-on-Avon,
where he established a Hunt Club, which, like the
Tarporley Hunt Club in Cheshire, commenced its
meetings on the first Monday in November. He

had also kennels at Meriden, near Coventry, for the Woodlands. He stayed there till the fox coverts wanted a little rest, then the hounds returned to Sundorne Castle, and great must have been the rejoicing of the Shropshire Squires when the flag on Haughmond Hill proclaimed to the countryside that Will Barrow (so celebrated for his view halloa) and his hounds were once more in sight of the Wrekin, though no doubt Will and his pack would be as much missed in Warwickshire as they would be joyfully welcomed in Shropshire.

Of Mr. Corbet's merit as a fox-hunter it is need-less to write. We may say that he hunted both Shropshire and Warwickshire with *great* success, and when he left Warwickshire he was esteemed a perfect "Master of the Art" of fox-hunting, and it will not be disputed if we say that no one of his day knew more of the good *and bad* properties of a hound than he did, and though he certainly was not a hard rider, seldom jumping a fence but by getting off his horse and turning him over, he managed to see a great deal of a run, and generally

knew more of the work of each hound than many
of those who were with them through the run, and
who only took them as a pack, without looking to
individual merits. He was, we believe, the first to
separate the sex of hounds in the field; was a
noted breeder of hounds, and spared no trouble in
the improvement of his pack. His favourite hound
was Trojan, a name that will be remembered by
Salopian fox-hunters for years to come, as at every
convivial meeting there was the toast 'with fox-
hunters of "one cheer more for the blood of Trojan."
There is a story told that this hound came as a
" waif and a stray" to the kennels at Sundorne,
and that no one knew where he came from, but that
he was so good-looking that he was taken out
hunting, and then his excellent qualities were discovered, and he was largely bred from, both by
Mr. Corbet and Sir Richard Puleston, as well as
other leading breeders of hounds in England.

Mr. Corbet, we find from his hound lists, also
bred from Lord Fitzwilliam's Fatal, Viper, Hero,
Layman, Pontiff, Tipler, and Actor, Sir R. Puleston's

Gainer, Dromo, Triumph, Dexter, and Trouncer, Sir Thomas Mostyn's Hannibal.

His pack in 1807 was reinforced by Rally, Venus, Marchioness, Duchess, Darlington, Lawyer, Leicester, Lowther, Rally, Bedford, Baroness, Hero, and Hardwick, from Prees kennels, probably when Mr. Hill gave up his hounds ; also by Bluster and Gameboy from Lord Southampton's.

In his hound book of 1807-8, we only find Driver, Dasher, Tryal (*sic*), Turpin, Tragedy, Thœtis, Trusty, and Tawdry by Trojan. In this book there is a Trojan who is described as by Driver out of Gladness. Mr Corbet bred a good deal from Driver, and in 1807 he had nine couples in his kennel by him.

Unfortunately Mr. Corbet's fox-hunting diary is either lost or mislaid, and thus we lose many valuable and interesting records of fox-hunting in those early days.

We have before us a very curious old picture of Mr. Corbet's hounds running a fox in view up Haughmond Hill, with the tower on the top, probably much as it is now. This is said to have been painted in the last century. All the scarlet coats have green collars of the same shade as those now worn by the members of the Tarporley Hunt Club.

Mr. Corbet gave up his hounds, which he kept for so many years without a subscription, in 1812, when he sold his 70 couples to Lord Middleton for the large price of 1,200 guineas. It was then, we believe, that Mr. Pelham took the hounds, with Ned Bate as his huntsman. We do not know a great deal about his success as a master of fox hounds, but we believe it was *not* very great, as in the first place, he only had a pack of hounds made up of drafts from Sir Richard Puleston's and other packs, which could not be made efficient in the time he had the hounds, and besides this, he cared nothing at all about hunting, and when his hounds found a fox he usually went off as fast as he could go in the opposite direction.

Mr. Pelham was quite a character, and many good stories are told of him ; as for instance, that he was once discovered breaking stones by the side of the

road *to see how much work a man could do in a day.*
His eccentricity was occasionally of a very practical
kind, as it is recorded that when he was a candidate
for the Parliamentary seat of the Borough of
Shrewsbury, his mode of canvassing the electors was
by walking along the middle of each street slapping
his breeches pocket ; need we say he was elected by
the free and independent electors. His shrewdness
also on another occasion satisfied a commission which
was making some impertinent enquiries about his
capacities for managing his own affairs, when, as the
story goes, he was asked how many legs a sheep
had ? which he answered by asking, dead or alive ?
He had the reputation of being a kind-hearted man,
a considerate landlord, and a sincere friend of the
working man.

When Mr. Pelham retired in 1817, John Mytton,
of Halston, took the country, which he hunted from
home with the aid of a " series " of hacks, including
that part of the Albrighton country which Sir
Richard Puleston had hunted, but which he now did
not require, as he had got hold of the Carden side

of his own country when Squire Leche gave it up.

Mr. Mytton's huntsman was John Craggs, who was afterwards killed by a fall from his horse in Halston's stable-yard ; *young* Ned Bate and Richard Jones, both excellent horsemen, being his whippers-in. All we know of Mr. Mytton's hounds and hunting establishment comes from the writings of Nimrod, who tells us his hounds were all sorts and sizes, but they must have been able to scurry along, or the Squire of Halston would have " ended " them either with a rope or his horse's hoofs.

Nimrod lived a great deal under John Mytton's most hospitable roof, and tells us of his horses and hounds, but is rather silent about the sport he showed. He says all the best runs with Mr. Mytton's hounds were from coverts in his own neighbourhood with travelling foxes from the Welsh hills ; one of these ran nearly to Ellesmere, and from there to Brynkinalt, and was killed near Lansillin. Three horses were killed by this run.

This hunting arrangement, however, only lasted to the year 1823, and then the gentlemen of Shropshire built kennels and stables about two miles from the town of Shrewsbury on the Whitchurch road, at an expense of £1,500, and invited Sir Bellingham Graham to hunt the country. Sir Bellingham's hunting establishment was all that could be desired; his stud of horses was magnificent, and by his personal influence he gave an impetus to fox-hunting in Shropshire, which lasted for a great many years. For the first two years of his management Sir Bellingham hunted the Albrighton country much as Mytton had done; but *now* a great deal of enthusiasm had grown up about fox-hunting, and the residents in Shropshire and Staffordshire countries who had hunting studs were much displeased that he should go away from their side for a time, and leave all the hunters in their part of the country idle in their boxes, so the end of it was that Sir Bellingham gave up the Albrighton country and confined his hunting to Shropshire.

Sir Bellingham was evidently an able adminstrator as far as fox-hunting was concerned, and well knew how to select his lieutenants; he it was who brought

x

Will Staples, son of old Tom Staples, Lord Middleton's huntsman, into Shropshire, as well as Jack Wrigglesworth, Tom Flint, and Joe Maiden, who was in after years so well known with the Cheshire. Sir Bellingham hunted his own hounds in a way that has possibly never been excelled. He was among the first and fastest horsemen England ever produced, and it was said of him that during the two seasons he hunted Leicestershire there was not a single instance of his not being *well* with his hounds, and right ably was he supported by that good sportsman Will Staples, of whom it is said that no man in England could follow the twisting and turnings of a hound to avoid the lash as well as he could. Sir Bellingham seems to have left behind him a reputation as a horseman and sportsman, which certainly up to his time beat the record, and in our early days we were constantly hearing his praises sung as a fox-hunter and breeder of hounds— certainly, neither trouble nor expense was spared over his kennel. We have one of his hound lists before us of the year 1818, and the tale it tells must, we think, bear out

our statement. Even in those non-railway days he
searched England's kennels through for good fox
hound blood. Among his pack we find Hymen
from Mr. Farquarson's, Sparkler and Barmaid by
Sir Thomas Mostyn's Lucifer, Lashwood and
Daflodil by his Lazarus, Tell Tale by Lord Fitz-
William's Transit, Raffle by his Lifter, Woldsman by
Mr. Osbaldeston's Dreadnought ; he also had
hounds by Mr. Lane-Fox's Tyrant and Palafox, the
Duke of Beaufort's Justice, Lord Lonsdale's Fair-
play, Jailer, Guardsman, Jester, Raymond, and
General; Lord Foley's Chaser, Regent and Dexter ;
Duke of Rutland's Lazarus and Wonder ; Sir Mark
Sykes' Dragon and Woodman ; Mr. Villebois'
Grapler ; Lord Vernon's Radnor ; Mr. Heron's
Bedford, Bruiser, Contract and Racer ; Lord
Darlington's Governor and Gulliver ; Duke of
Grafton's Rhoderick ; Lord Yarborough's Wildboy ;
Lord Althorp's Charm and Outlaw ; Mr. Hanbury's
Pillager ; Mr. Warde's Ganymede. In all there were
seventy couples of hounds in his kennels, and if they
were not good enough to hunt a fox, the fault cannot

be in the blood selected ; but we have no doubt the
sport Sir Bellingham showed quite satisfied those
who hunted with him ; but after a time he yearned
after a grass country, so in 1826 he sold his hounds
to the country and went into Leicestershire.

Sir Bellingham was, without doubt, a great loss
to Shropshire when he left it.   He was said to be
one of the most generous of men, and a most agree-
able companion.   As a yachtsman, too, he took high
honours, and was Vice-Commodore of the Cowes
Squadron.   He died of old age in 1866.

Then the Shropshire Hounds were managed by a
Committee, the principal members being Sir Edward
Smythe, Mr. Lloyd, of Aston, and Mr. Smythe
Owen.   This arrangement, however, lasted only a
few years, and in 1833 the country was divided, Sir
Rowland Hill—afterwards Lord Hill—taking the
North, with Will Staples as his huntsman, Mr.
Smythe Owen the South, with kennels at Condover.

North Shropshire has always been so much mixed
up with the Wynnstay country that everyone who
hunts in one ought to be interested in the other, and

LORD HILL AND WILL STAPLES.

this is our reason and excuse for adding what we much fear will be considered a very imperfect rider to the preceding chapters, our only object being to show briefly how it came about that any part of Shropshire was hunted from this side, and this side hunted by Shropshire hounds.

Through the kindness of Mr. Frank Bibby, we are able to give some extracts from Will Staples' diary, of whom, by the way, a good story was told by the Vicar of Shawbury, who married him. Will Staples asked in the vestry, " *What's the damage*, Sir ?" With a pleasant laugh, which was joined in by all the large wedding party, the Vicar answered : " You will find that out soon enough " ; a prophecy which probably came true.

Will Staples' Diary, 1828.

October 22nd. "Found an old fox in the Twemlows. Went away directly for Ash, 55 minutes to ground at Iscoed in the main earth."

Dec. 17th. " Met at Halston. Mrs. Mytton being very ill, Mr. Lloyd did not intend to hunt the covers at Halston. Mr. Mytton, however, insisted.

Killed one directly, and in the meantime a fox was viewed away. We got the hounds on the line and ran for Hardwick, thence to Ellesmere Town, and ran him very quick to Kilhendre, where he was killed.   1 hour 25 minutes."

The following entry is given as marking an age happily now past.

Dec. 24th.   " Met at Twemlows.   Drew the covers blank ; found in Kingston Hill (at the time the hounds were running the fox in the cover, there was a bull bait under the Hill), eventually to ground on the Grotto Hill."

Dec. 27th.   " Met at Eaton Mascot.   When drawing the Dingle a fox was viewed, which ran to Pitchford, and was killed after a first-rate run of an hour and 40 minutes ; only one check, about a minute.   These mentioned were with the hounds the whole of the time—Mr. Lloyd, of Aston, Mr. Henry Lyster, Mr. Thomas Beck, Mr. Farmer, myself, and the two whippers-in."

Jan. 10th, 1829.   " Finish of the hunt week ; met at Boreatton ; found and came away for Nescliff ;

hunted him over a very fine country to the Severn, which he crossed, when hounds were stopped. They killed 25 brace this season."

November 2nd, 1829. " Met at Mr. Matthews, of Montford, found on Nescliff, ran about for some time and killed one on the point of the rock. When I got to them there were three hounds hanging down the rock by their hold of the fox ; pulled Joker and Woodman up, but the other, Welcome, lost her hold and fell thirty or forty yards down the rock and was killed. As I was going round the hill to get the bitch that had fallen, another fox came bounding off the side of the rock, and the hounds with me caught sight of him and killed him close by the bitch that had fallen."

We give the following two runs, though they were not from meets we are now especially interested in, simply because they were very good ones :

November 27th, 1830. " Met at High Hatton and were going to draw Morgan's Pool, when the hounds went away with a scent over the Hodnet and Shrewsbury road ; ultimately, when they were by Mrs. Dickins' Farm at Holdbrook, they caught view of him and killed him in grand style ; the time from finding to killing him was two hours and five minutes, only one check more than a minute."

December 8th. " At Chetwynd, after killing ' one' and running to ground they found an old fox on Ercal Heath, which the hounds killed in the open in as good style as ever a fox was killed in. The run was one hour, and the ground gone over was from nine to ten miles, and a very severe country it was. So severe was the pace that the horses could not live with the hounds. I had the pleasure of seeing the hounds four or five fields ahead of me like a flock of pigeons, and I was without company for a long time till Captain Turner was kind enough to come and join me. When we came to Stoke Heath a good many came up, and as the hounds were going away again, many more came along the road and joined us ; had there been no roads there would have been only Captain Turner and ' myself' at the Heath."

Various incidents are quaintly recorded, as of

Henry Lyster, Esq., killing "his little mare by leaping her into a pit; supposed to have broke her neck."

February, 1831, the meet was altered "to accommodate Sir Rowland Hill, Bt., as there was a call *in* the house."

March 16th, 1831. " Met at the Twemlows. Going to Lighteach a fox jumped out of a pit hole. When the hounds were put on the scent, they went away like a shot out of a gun, and you might have covered them with a sheet. Not knowing the country, I can't say what parishes they were in. Then back by Tilstock by the place where he was found, and up to Prees Village, where we killed him. The run was one hour and twenty-five minutes, and all the time going a good racing pace; the country being very heavy, horses could not live with them, but got to them by roads, and as well as they could. There were many gentlemen out of Cheshire and Mr. Wickstead's country, and they were highly delighted with the day's sport."

March 22nd, 1831. The diary records when they

Y

met at Whittington. " Mr. Wynn was Master, as
Sir Edward, Smythe Owen, and Mr. Lloyd were
not out. Mr. Wynn rode his chestnut horse, and
the humped-backed mare as hack, and ' he ' died on
the Thursday week following."

Unfortunately the diaries between this time and
1835 are lost, the year of the season 1833-34 would
have been specially interesting, as during that
season the Shropshire Hounds hunted a great deal of
Sir Richard Puleston's country. which he had just
vacated, and no one supplied his place until the
following year.

We have Sir Rowland Hill's meets for 1833-34,
and those that are now Wynnstay meets are
Oteley, Queen's Head, Petton, Nescliff, Iscoed
Park, Penley Green, Halston, Alan Sadler's,
Brynypys, Shocklach Village. Gredington, Boreatton.
and Emral.

Shropshire was divided in 1833, Sir Rowland
Hill took North Shropshire with Will Staples as
huntsman, while Mr. Smythe Owen took the south,
having his kennels at Condover, and for eight

seasons fox-hunting prospered under this arrangement, which appears to outsiders a most desirable one. Unfortunately, as we have said, we know nothing of the sport at this time, which would have a great interest for us, as, on Sir Richard Puleston's retirement, the Shropshire hunted a great deal of his country, and we see from Will Staples' diary that the Shropshire hunted Bettisfield, Petton, Iscoed, &c. A great deal of this they continued to hunt until Sir Watkin was master of the Wynnstay Hounds, and then he hunted all the places we have just named, besides going in 1847 into the *heart* of North Shropshire, which the Wynnstay pack continues to hunt till the present day.

We are much amused at Will Staples' quaint expressions; and his diary, which he evidently never thought of anyone seeing but himself, has a peculiar interest on this account.

On 14th November, 1835, we have a good illustration of this:—" Met at Ercall Village; in the burst, the Rev. John Hill had a fall, with his foot hanging in the stirrup; very fortunately his horse stood still, till he got released; soon after, I *seconded* the *motion, flat as a flounder.*"

21st November, 1835. "Met at Iscoed, found in Bubney Gorse, crossed to the plantation facing the park palings, then went down the side land meadows to where the brooks meet, and where the three counties come each of them to a corner, Shropshire, Cheshire, and Flintshire; we then went in the direction of the Wyches, then turned to the right over the Whitchurch and Malpas roads, and ran in the direction of Cholmondeley, crossed the Chester road not far from the Blue Cap Public House, and went to the Bickerton Hills, where we lost him. The ground we went over was thirteen or fourteen miles; some very hard running and some hunting, still going a pretty good pace. The run was one hour and twenty minutes."

28th November. "Met at Petton." Of the second run, the diary says, "It was tip-top pace, and only one check and that momentary in middle."

5th December, when they met at Oteley they had "a good hunting run to Hardwick, then to North-

wood, past Bettisfield Springs to Braden Heath;
lost him in the Duke's woods."

23rd January, 1836. Met Iscoed. "We found,
without doubt, the same fox we had such a good run
with the last time we met there, 21st November ; we
did not quite reach the Bickerton Hills; the time was
one hour twelve minutes, and Sir Rowland would not
draw again as he had intended going to the Twemlows."

February 19th. "Met at Iscoed ; found in Bubney Gorse and took the same line of country as he
took twice before, till he came to the lower end of
the Wyches, then, when going for Shocklach Gorse,
he was headed back, and we killed him by the salt
mine, one hour ten minutes. Mr. Leche's hounds
were drawing some part of the Wyches, and two
couples of his hounds joined *us*, and we shut them
up at a farm-house close by. Sir Harry Mainwaring,
his son, and Joe Maiden, were out with us and
several of the gentlemen. Joe Maiden bought the
chestnut horse of Mr. Powell, of Preston Brock-
hurst. Sir Rowland came from London last night,
and was hunting to-day."

No London and North Western Railway then; no doubt his own carriage with post horses or a "yellow agony" all the way from Shrewsbury to London and back.

14th November, 1837. "Met at Petton; this morning we almost received the death blow; Sir Rowland going to give up his hounds, everyone with his face as long as a fiddle. 'Will, is this true?' was the cry of the morning. Half an hour later, when the word, Gone away from Burlton Wood was the cry, everyone seemed to regain their countenance so long as a hound could speak to the scent; when the fox was lost, then came the old story. Old Mr. S. Denston came to me and said, 'This will kill me'; said another, 'I must sell my horses'; 'What are we to do,' from all sides. I was glad when I got home from the melancholy scene."

January 26th, 1839. "Met at the Black Birches, found a good fox on Shawbury Heath; had an extraordinary run of some hours, crossing the Severn three times. Near Shilton Gate the fox turned into a lane, and allowed me to take him up before

the hounds ; when I put him down he could not
stand. We were running him — hours — minutes,
sometimes going top pace, at others very pretty
hunting ; no hounds could do their work better. At
the death were H. B. Clive, Esq., R. A. Slaney,
Esq., T. Eyton, Esq., Hon. H. Powys Edwards,
T. Evans on Dr. Walmsley's horse went well,
myself, Will and Peter."

February 12th. " Met at Cloverley, when they
had a run at a good pace. *Note*—Sir Rowland
Hill mounted our new master, Isaac Hodgson, Esq."

Probably Mr. Hodgson had not then entered on
the duty of master of the Shropshire Hounds, but
would commence his reign in the autumn of this
year ; he was a true sportsman, and would no doubt
make a good and popular master, but as far as we
can recollect, did not continue in office for more than
two seasons, when he came to reside at Broughton
Hall in the Wynnstay country. He had a *bad* man
to follow in Lord Hill, who was universally respected,
and whose expenditure over his household and
kennel was on a most liberal scale ; this, as we can

plainly see, would make it difficult for him or anyone else to follow Lord Hill.

22nd March, 1839. " Met at Doddington ; found and went away for Crewe, round the house and gardens at Crewe Hall, then to Wistaston ; here we viewed him close before the hounds, and the gentlemen riding and halloaing ; got the hounds' heads up and lost five minutes by it. When the hounds settled again he went up to Crewe Station. Here I had the good luck to stop the hounds till one of the trains passed ; then crossed to Crewe Wood, hunted him from there, and got up to him at Basford Wood, then turned short to the right (here my horse stopped) and went to ground in a sand hole close to Gresty Green, the hounds close to him at the time. The run was two hours and ten minutes, and over twenty miles of ground. I am sorry to say my horse died as soon as he got to *the* Styche."

January 29th, 1840. They met at the Twemlows and had a run and kill of an hour and ten minutes. *Footnote*—" Mr. Hodgson was not out, he went to see Sir Richard Puleston's harriers at Northwood."

February 10th, 1840. "Met at Iscoed; found in Bubney and Bettisfield Springs, ran by Hanmer, Gredington, Penley, going in the direction of Emral, but turning to the right he made his way to Gredington; here we got close to him. He then went through Bettisfield Park, Mr. Hodgson and myself viewed him going out of the Park; unfortunately the hounds came to a check with the deer and sheep crossing the line. By that means the fox got a great way before us. We hunted him to the Fenns, then turned to the left by the London Apprentice Public House, as if going to the Wyches; here we were obliged to stop the hounds, for it was getting dusk and horses were beaten. Well's mare was down dead beaten. ˙ Mr. G. Clay was riding Losbin, Mr. Matthews, Drummer, and Mr. J. Minor his grey horse; these were all that saw the run; it was one hour forty-five minutes. *Footnote*—the Queen was married this day."

October 2nd, 1840. After relating the sport of that day there is a *footnote*—" I am sorry to say the remainder of this season is *lost* through my neglect. Killed 22 brace. 8 weeks' frost."

z

November 5th, 1841. "When the hounds met at
High Hatton a chimney-sweep viewed a fox crossing
the turnpike road. Mr. H. Clive gave me the signal
by blowing his horn.   I think at the same time he
was doubtful whether the fellow in black knew a fox ;
but the hounds soon told us the sweep was right.
However, he was lost at Hawkstone.   Mr. Hodgson
was out on this day."

Mr. Clive appears to have taken an active part in
the management of the hounds in the field, as on the
16th November he gained permission to draw
Shavington, which they did that day "as the field
was small ;" but there was no fox there.

The diary ends March, 1842.   It is a most
valuable addition to the history of fox-hunting in
this country, and but for the loss of the years from
1831 to 1835, it would have far more interest for
fox-hunters in our country.

When Mr. Hodgson gave up the Shropshire
Hounds, they were again hunted by a Committee,
with Henry Clive as Field Master, and this management, we believe, continued till the close of the

season of 1844-45, when Mr. Eyton, for two seasons, was Master; and at the end of this time, 1846-47, the Shropshire Hounds and the kennels at Lee Bridge were untenanted for a good many years. It was then that Sir Watkin Wynn, by arrangement, became possessed of so fine a part of the Shropshire country, most of which is still hunted by the Wynn-stay Hounds.

We have no wish to carry further this sketch of the history of fox-hunting in Shropshire, but we desired to tell how it came about that this side of the country was hunted by the Shropshire Hounds, and how to this day some of the Shropshire country is hunted from Wynnstay.

Willingly would we write of the joyous days when the present Lord Hill hunted the Shropshire country with such unbounded success, but alas! we have not the materials, though we do know from our own experience of him in the hunting-field that, as far as we are able to judge, no man was ever better qualified than he was to be either a master of fox hounds, or to hunt them.

Perhaps we ought to add a note of congratulation both to the hunting men of Shropshire and the Wynnstay country on the happy prospects before them with two such munificent men as masters of their respective countries as Mr. Heywood Lonsdale and the present Sir Watkin Wynn. There is no doubt that fox-hunting will flourish, and be a bond of union between landlord and tenant, till those good old times return when the farmer may again say,

" Now missus, sin' the markets be doing moderate well,
   I've welly made my mind up to buy a nag mysel' ;
   For to keep a farmer's spirits up 'gainst things be getting
      low,
   There's nothing like fox-hunting and a rattling *Tally-ho*."

FINIS.

SIR W. WYNN.

www.ingramcontent.com/pod-product-compliance
Lightning Source LLC
Chambersburg PA
CBHW030513100426
42813CB00001B/23